Cultivating
the Mind of Love

Cultivating the Mind of Love

The Practice of Looking Deeply
in the Mahayana Buddhist Tradition

THICH NHAT HANH

Foreword by Natalie Goldberg

PARALLAX
P
PRESS

Parallax Press
Berkeley, California

Parallax Press
P.O. Box 7355
Berkeley, California 94707

Cover and book design by Legacy Media, Inc.
Cover painting, "Looking Deeply," oil on canvas, by Barbara Zaring.

In Buddhist texts, consciousness is said to be a field, a plot of land
in which every kind of seed has been planted—seeds of suffering,
happiness, joy, sorrow, fear, anger, and hope. The quality of our
life depends on which of these seeds we water. The practice of
mindfulness is to recognize each seed as it sprouts and to water the
most wholesome seeds whenever possible.

Library of Congress Cataloging-in-Publication Data
Nhât Hanh, Thích
    Cultivating the mind of love: the practice of looking deeply in
the Mahayana Buddhist tradition/Thich Nhat Hanh; foreword by
Natalie Goldberg.
        p. cm.
    Includes bibliographical references.
    ISBN 0-938077-70-8 (pbk.)
    1. Mahayana Buddhism—Doctrines. 2. Religious life Mahayana
Buddhism. I. Title.
BQ7410.N43 1995
294.3'92—dc20
                                                    95-38078
                                                    CIP

4   5   6   7   8   9   10   /   03   02   01   00   99

Contents

Foreword

I am continually amazed at how Thich Nhat Hanh is able to translate the Buddhist tradition into everyday life and make it relevant and helpful for so many people. *Cultivating the Mind of Love* just might be my favorite book of his, because it's about one of our all-time favorite subjects and the one we're all confused about: Love.

In June 1992 I was fortunate enough to attend the retreat in France where he gave the Dharma talks that comprise these pages. I will never forget how I felt listening to him. Here was a Zen master, committed to mindfulness, examining the nature of love. What is it? How do we handle it? Who are we in this state? What do we really want? We've all been struck by love, but what do we do with it? Most of us tumble willy-nilly into it and lose clear perception, perspective, or common sense. Often what began with joy becomes a pitfall. But in the Dharma Nectar Hall in Plum Village, I listened to Thich Nhat Hanh, who stood steady in love's torrential waves, scrutinized it, and grounded it in deep practice.

Hearing Thây (Vietnamese for "teacher"), I felt for the first time that sanity had entered the realm of love. Each morning he lectured for two hours and I eagerly came early to the zendo and sat right in front of him. I was ready to have those teachings poured into me. It was a revelation to realize I did not necessarily have to be tossed about when Cupid's arrow hit. I thought how compassionate he was to try to explain love's source to a Western world dazed and dazzled by the promise of romance and song lyrics full of yearning.

He talked about the *Diamond*, *Avatamsaka*, and *Lotus Sutras*. Then halfway into each morning, he switched the subject and told us another episode of his falling in love as a young monk with a nun. "Falling in love is an accident," he said. "Think about it: the expression 'falling'; you trip into it. It was not supposed to happen. After all, I was a monk; she was a nun." He did not act upon it in a capricious way, as we normally do. He examined these strong feelings with awareness and then, more than forty years later, he shared the benefit of that with us. I realized he was teaching us how to love well.

I flip through my notebook now and see the notes I took then. They seem to glimmer off the page:

"Your first love has no beginning or end. Your first love is not your first love, and it is not your last. It is just love. It is one with everything."

"The present moment is the only moment available to us, and it is the door to all moments."

"No coming. No going. Everything is pretending to be born and to die."

"This self has no self."

"It is okay to suffer in the process of love."

Everyone in the hall felt the instant recognition of what he said, though it often bypassed our logical brain and went directly into our hearts. Yes, we thought, love is much more-dimensional than chocolate bonbons on Valentine's Day.

One morning I had an idea and wrote a note to Thây: "Why don't all of us write for half an hour about our first love, examining those feelings—the texture, the light and dark we felt." I thought it was a great opportunity to investigate our experience. I realized then that the work of a Zen master is also the work of a writer—to take nothing for granted but to live deeply and feel the life we have been given. It is also the work of everyone if we are to bring peace to this world. It is our chance to glimpse the interconnected nature of all things and how our "first love has no beginning or end." The next day Thây read my note aloud to the Sangha and encouraged them all to write. I encourage the readers of this book to do the same.

In Taos, New Mexico, where I live and where a small Sangha gathers every Wednesday night to meditate, walk, recite the precepts, and share tea, we now also read aloud two pages from this book at each meeting. It is our hope to digest it gradually, so what we learn becomes rooted. We know this simple book can change the face of our interactions, our motives, our minds.

I urge you to take in Thich Nhat Hanh's words slowly, the way molasses pours in winter, so you will nourish your whole being and so we may walk more kindly on this Earth.

Natalie Goldberg
Taos, New Mexico
June 1995

Cultivating
the Mind of Love

ONE

Dharma Rain

Three years ago, I gave a series of talks about my first love. Everyone at Plum Village, the community where I live and practice in France, was very concentrated. They were listening with the whole of their being, not just with their intellects. Seeds of love and understanding buried deep within their consciousness were touched, and I could see that they were listening not just to my talk, but to their own as well. When a subject is interesting, you don't need to work hard to listen. Concentration is there without effort, and understanding is born from concentration.

When you listen to a Dharma talk, just allow the rain of the Dharma to penetrate the soil of your consciousness. Don't think too much; don't argue or compare. Playing with words and ideas is like trying to catch rain in buckets. Just allow your consciousness to receive the rain, and the seeds buried deep within will have a chance to be watered.

Consciousness in Buddhism is said to be composed of two parts—"store consciousness" (*alayavijñana*) and "mind consciousness" (*manovijñana*). In our store consciousness are buried all the seeds, representing everything we have ever done, experienced, or perceived. When a seed is watered, it manifests in our mind consciousness. The work of meditation is to cultivate the garden of our store consciousness. As gardener, we have to trust the land, knowing that all seeds of love and understanding, seeds of enlightenment and happiness, are already there. That is why we don't have to think too hard or take notes during a Dharma talk. We only need to be there, to allow the seeds of love and understanding that are buried deep within us to be watered. It is not just the teacher who is giving the Dharma talk. The violet bamboo, the yellow chrysanthemum, and the golden sunset are all speaking at the same time. Anything that waters these deepest seeds in our store consciousness is the true Dharma.

When a woman becomes pregnant, something happens in her body and also in her spirit. The presence of the baby in her transforms her life, and a new energy arises that allows her to do things she previously could not. She smiles and trusts humanity more, and becomes a deep source of joy and happiness for others. Even when she feels unwell, there is a genuine peace within her, and others can feel it.

We who practice meditation can learn from this. There is a baby Buddha in our store consciousness, and we have to give him or her a chance to be born. When we touch our baby Buddha—the seeds of understanding and love that are buried within us—we become filled with *bodhichitta*, the mind of enlightenment, the mind of love. From that moment on, everything we do or say nourishes the baby Buddha within us, and we are filled with joy, confidence, and energy. According to Mahayana Buddhism, awakening our bodhichitta, touching our mind of enlightenment, our mind of love, is the moment the practice begins.

Our mind of love may be buried deep in our store consciousness, under many layers of forgetfulness and suffering. The teacher's role is to help us water it, to help it manifest. In Zen Buddhism, the teacher may propose a *kung an* (*koan* in Japanese), and if teacher and student are lucky and skillful enough, the student's mind of enlightenment will be touched. The student buries the kung an deep in his store consciousness, and his practice is to nourish the kung an, concentrating only on the kung an even while sweeping the floor, washing the dishes, or listening to the bell. He entrusts his kung an to his store consciousness, just as a woman who is pregnant trusts her body to nourish her baby.

Deep understanding of the Dharma takes place slowly. If you tell me you already understand, I feel a little pessimistic. You think you understand, but you may not have understood. If you say you do not understand, I feel more optimistic. Listen with the whole of your being. Allow yourself to be fully present, and the rain of the Dharma will water the deepest seeds in your store consciousness. If the seed of understanding is watered, tomorrow while you are washing the dishes or looking at the blue sky, that seed may spring forth, and the fruits of love and understanding will grow beautifully from your store consciousness.

TWO

First Love

She was twenty years old when I met her. We were at the Temple of Complete Awakening in the highlands of Vietnam. I had just given a course on basic Buddhism, and the abbot of the temple asked, "Thây, why don't you take a break and stay with us here for a few days before returning to Saigon?" I said, "Sure, why not?"

I had been in the village that day, helping a group of young people rehearse a play they were going to perform for Tết, the Vietnamese lunar New Year. More than anything else, I wanted to help renew Buddhism in my country, to make it relevant to the needs of the young people. I was twenty-four, full of creative energy, an artist and a poet. It was a time of war with the French, and many people were dying. One Dharma brother of mine, Thây Tam Thuong, had just been killed. As I was walking up the steps to return to the temple, I saw a nun standing there, looking out onto the nearby hills. Seeing her standing like that was like a fresh breeze blowing across my face. I had seen many nuns before, but I had never had a feeling like that.

For you to understand, I have to share some experiences I'd had many years earlier. When I was nine, I saw on the cover of a magazine an image of the Buddha sitting peacefully on the grass. Right away I knew that I wanted to be peaceful and happy like that. Two years later, when five of us were discussing what we wanted to be when we grew up, my brother Nho said, "I want to become a monk." It was a novel idea, but I knew I also wanted to become a monk. At least in part, it was because I had seen the image of the Buddha on the magazine. Young people are very open and very impressionable. I hope film and TV producers will take this to heart.

Six months after that, our class went on a field trip to Na Son Mountain. I had heard that a hermit lived there. I didn't know what a hermit was, but I felt I wanted to see him. I had heard people say that a hermit is someone dedicated to becoming peaceful and happy like a Buddha. We walked six miles to the mountain and then climbed for another hour, but when we arrived, our teachers told us that the hermit wasn't there. I was very disappointed. I didn't understand that hermits do not want to see many people. So when the rest of the class stopped for lunch, I continued uphill, hoping to encounter him on my own. Suddenly, I heard the sound of water dripping, and I followed that sound until I found a beautiful well nestled among the stones. When I looked down into it, I could see every pebble and every leaf at the bottom. I knelt down and drank the sparkling, clear water, and felt completely fulfilled. It was as if I were meeting the hermit face to face! Then I lay down and fell asleep.

When I woke up a few minutes later, I didn't know where I was. Then I remembered my classmates, and as I headed down to join them, a sentence came to my mind, not in Vietnamese, but in French: "*J'ai goûté l'eau la plus délicieuse du monde.*" ("I have tasted the most delicious water in the world.") My friends were relieved to see me, but I continued to think only about the hermit and the well. After they returned to playing, I ate my lunch in silence.

My brother was the first to become a monk, and everyone in our family was worried that the life of a monk would be too difficult. So I didn't tell them about my wish to follow the same path. But the seed within me continued to grow, and four years later my dream was realized. I became a novice monk at Tu Hiêu Pagoda, near the Imperial City of Huê, in central Vietnam.

THREE

The Advent of Mahayana Buddhism

During his lifetime, the Buddha gave most of his Dharma talks to monks and nuns, but he also taught kings, ministers, farmers, scavengers, and thousands of other lay men and women. Many sutras such as the *Ugradatta* and *Vimalakirti Sutras* are devoted to lay practice. When Anathapindika, a strong lay supporter of the Buddha and the Sangha, was given the teachings on emptiness and non-self, he understood them deeply, and he asked the Venerable Ananda to tell the Buddha that laypeople are capable of learning and practicing these wonderful teachings.

But in the centuries following the Buddha's life, the practice of the Dharma became the exclusive domain of monks and nuns, and laypeople were limited to supporting the ordained Sangha with food, shelter, clothing, and medicine. By the first century B.C.E., Buddhist practice had become so exclusively monastic that a reaction was inevitable. The *Ugradatta Sutra* was born in that context.

In the *Ugradatta Sutra*, three questions are asked: How does a monk (*bhikshu*; *bhikkhu* in Pali) practice? How does a lay *bodhisattva* practice? How does a lay bodhisattva practice so that he or she is equal to a monk or a nun? In this sutra, after hearing the Buddha speak, five hundred laypeople expressed their wish to become monks and nuns, but two hundred others, who had been able to produce the mind of enlightenment during the Buddha's Dharma talk, did not. Venerable Ananda asked Ugradatta, "Why don't you become a monk like us?" and Ugradatta said, "I don't need to become a monk. I can practice just as well as a layman."

That idea was developed to its utmost in the *Vimalakirti Nirdesha Sutra*. Vimalakirti, a layman who was far more advanced than any of the monks, nuns, or celestial bodhisattvas in the Buddha's retinue, pretends to be sick, and the Buddha asks Venerable Shariputra to go and inquire about him. Shariputra responds, "My lord, he is too eloquent and intelligent. Please ask someone else to go." The Buddha then asks Ananda and many other monks and bodhisattvas, but no one wants to visit Vimalakirti. Finally, Manjushri Bodhisattva accepts, and Vimalakirti demonstrates over and over that his insights are much deeper than Manjushri's or any other bodhisattva's. The appearance of Vimalakirti in the development of Mahayana Buddhism was natural. This sutra was a strong attack on the institution of monasticism, attempting to open it up so the monks and nuns would practice in a more open and engaged way for the whole of society and not just for themselves.

The *Vimalakirti Sutra* was so successful that there were sequels to it—one about a son of Vimalakirti, another about a daughter of Vimalakirti, and even one about the teachings of a woman who had been a prostitute. The point was that Buddhism could be taught by anyone who has realized his or her awakened mind. Even a prostitute, when she learns and practices the Dharma, can become the teacher of gods and men. In these sutras, the Mahayana ideal of the lay bodhisattva reached its highest expression. In the *Vimalakirti Sutra*, we see that illustrious monks like Shariputra and Mogallana are just lowly students when compared with bodhisattvas, those who are practicing for the benefit of everyone.

In the early *Prajñaparamita Sutras*, many sentences condemn the attitude of monks who practice only for themselves. In the *Astasahashrika Prajñaparamita Sutra* we read: "When the queen sleeps with a man who is not the king, although she may give birth to a child, that child cannot be described as having royal blood. Unless you are motivated by an enlightened mind and heart to practice as a bodhisattva for all beings, you are not truly the son or daughter of the Buddha. If you practice only for your own emancipation, you are not truly a son or daughter of the Buddha."

If monks and nuns did not open themselves up and practice for everyone, embracing the ideal of the bodhisattva, they were said to be "not true sons and daughters of the Buddha." In the *Ugradatta*, *Vimalakirti*, and early *Prajñaparamita Sutras*, Mahayana Buddhist thought is abundant and deep, but the tone of these sutras is still one of attack. It must have been difficult to get the attention of the monastic establishment, so taking an adversarial stance must have been necessary. But by the time of the *Saddharma Pundarika (Lotus) Sutra*, Mahayana Buddhism was already an institution with schools, temples, and a solid foundation—a kind of "protestant" Buddhist community of monks, nuns, and laypeople working closely together. So the tone of the *Lotus Sutra* is one of reconciliation. In the *Vimalakirti Sutra*, Shariputra is nothing, but in the *Lotus Sutra* the Buddha shows great love and care for Shariputra and all his monk and nun disciples. The *Lotus Sutra* is at the foundation of Mahayana Buddhism, because its tone of inclusiveness extends a friendly, loving hand to the traditional institutions of Buddhism.

FOUR

The Beauty of Spring

Please think about your own first love. Do it slowly, picturing how it came about, where it took place, what brought you to that moment. Recall that experience and look at it calmly and deeply, with compassion and understanding. You will discover many things you did not notice at the time. There is a kung an in the Zen tradition, "What was your face before your parents were born?" This is an invitation to go on a journey and discover your true self, your true face. Look deeply into your "first love" and try to see its true face. When you do, you will see that your "first love" may not really be the first, that your face when you were born may not have been your original face. If you look deeply, you will be able to see your true, original face, and your true first love. Your first love is still present, always here, continuing to shape your life. This is a subject for meditation.

When I met her, it was not exactly the first time we had met. Otherwise, how could it have happened so easily? If I had not seen the image of the Buddha on the magazine, our meeting would not have been possible. If she had not been a nun, I would not have loved her. There was a great peace in her, the fruit of sincere practice, that was not present in others. She had been practicing in her nunnery in Huê, and she appeared as peaceful as the Buddha sitting on the grass. My visit to the hermit, tasting the pure water of his well, was also part of our first meeting. The moment I saw her, I recognized in her everything I cherished.

She was in the highlands visiting her family, but as a nun she preferred to stay at the temple. She had heard about the course on basic Buddhism I had taught, so she expected to meet me, but I had not heard about her. When I got to the top of the stairs, I bowed and asked her name. We went inside to become acquainted. In every temple, there is a special seat for the abbot, and I had to sit there, because the abbot was away for a few days and had asked me to serve in his stead. I invited her to sit in front of me, but she sat off to the side. Members of the community never sit in front of the abbot. It is just the form. To see each other's faces, we had to turn our heads.

Her behavior as a nun was perfect—the way she moved, the way she looked, the way she spoke. She was quiet. She never said anything unless she was spoken to. She just looked down in front of her. I was shy, too. I never dared look at her for more than a second or two, and then I lowered my eyes again. After a few minutes, I said good-bye and went to my room. I didn't know what had happened, but I knew my peace had been disturbed. I tried writing a poem, but I couldn't compose even one line! So I began to read the poetry of others, hoping that would calm me down.

I read several poems by Nguyen Binh. He was longing for his mother and sister, and I felt the same way. When you become a monk at a young age, you miss your family. In Vietnam, before reading this type of poetry, you burn incense, light candles, and then chant the poem. I remember that I had a few tears in my eyes when I chanted this in classical Chinese:

> Night is here.
> The wind and the rain announce the news
> that spring is coming.
> Still I sleep alone, my dream not yet realized.
>
> Flower petals falling
> seem to understand my dreams and aspirations.
> They touch the ground of spring
> in perfect silence.

I continued to recite poetry all afternoon and evening. I thought about my family and chanted aloud, trying to relieve the feelings in me that I could not understand. At six o'clock, a student from the class I had taught knocked on my door and invited me to supper. Before leaving, the abbot had asked her to come every day to prepare lunch and dinner.

The young nun and I ate in silence, and then we shared a pot of tea and spoke quietly together. She told me how she had become a nun, where she trained before entering the Buddhist Institute in Huê, and what she was studying. She continued to look down, looking up only when I asked her a question. She looked like Kwan Yin—calm, compassionate, and beautiful. From time to time, I looked at her, but for not long. If she saw me looking at her like that, it would have been impolite. After ten or fifteen minutes, I excused myself and went into the Buddha Hall to practice sitting meditation and chanting.

The next morning, I went into the hall again for sitting and chanting, and, after a few minutes, I heard her voice beside me. After we finished chanting, we left the hall and had another conversation before breakfast. That morning, she went to see her family, and I was alone in the temple. In the afternoon, I went to the village to help the young people rehearse their play. When I returned, climbing up the steps, I saw her again standing in front of the temple, looking out at the tea plantation on the hillside. We had dinner together, and afterwards, I read her some of my poetry. Then I went to my room and read poetry alone. Nothing had changed from the day before, but inside I understood. I knew that I loved her. I only wanted to be with her—to sit near her and contemplate her.

I didn't sleep much that night. The next morning after sitting and chanting, I proposed that we go to the kitchen and build a fire. It was cold and she agreed. We had a cup of tea together, and I tried my best to tell her that I loved her. I said many things, but I couldn't say that. I spoke about other things, hoping she would understand. She listened intently, with compassion, and then she whispered, "I don't understand a word you've said."

But the next day she told me she understood. It was difficult for me, but much more difficult for her. My love was like a storm, and she was being caught and carried away by the energy of the storm. She had tried to resist, but couldn't, and she finally accepted. We both needed compassion. We were young, and we were being swept away. We had the deepest desire to be a monk and a nun— to carry forward what we had been cherishing for a long time—yet we were caught by love.

That night I wrote a poem:

> Spring comes slowly and quietly
> to allow winter to withdraw
> slowly and quietly.
> The color of the mountain this afternoon
> is tinged with nostalgia.
> The terrible war flower
> has left her footprints—
> countless petals of separation and death
> in white and violet.
>
> Very tenderly, the wound opens itself in the
> depths of my heart.
> Its color is the color of blood,
>
> its nature the nature of separation.
> The beauty of spring blocks my way.

How could I find another path up the
mountain?

I suffer so. My soul is frozen.
My heart vibrates like the fragile string of a lute
left out in a stormy night.
Yes, it is there. Spring has really come.
But the mourning is heard
clearly, unmistakably,
in the wonderful sounds of the birds.
The morning mist is already born.
The breeze of spring in its song
expresses both my love and my despair.
The cosmos is so indifferent. Why?
To the harbor, I came alone,
and now I leave alone.

There are so many paths leading to the homeland.
They all talk to me in silence. I invoke the
Absolute.

Spring has come
to every corner of the ten directions.
Its song, alas, is only the song
of departure.

I wrote this poem for relief. How could we continue as a monk and a nun and still preserve this precious love?

Monks do not usually share stories like this, but I think it is important to do so. Otherwise, how will the younger generation know what to do when they are struck? As a monk, you are not supposed to fall in love, but sometimes love is stronger than your determination. This story is about precepts, mindfulness, Sangha, bodhichitta, and transformation.

FIVE

The Better Way to Catch a Snake

In the *Sutra on Knowing the Better Way to Catch a Snake*, the Buddha shows us the way to see reality clearly without getting stuck in concepts or notions. I had studied the *Diamond Sutra* for many years before encountering the *Snake Sutra*, and I was happy to learn that the simile of the raft and the "thundering silence" statement made by the Buddha have their roots in this early sutra.

According to the *Snake Sutra*, we have to be careful when we study the Dharma, because if we understand it incorrectly, we can cause harm to ourselves and others. The Buddha said that understanding the Dharma is like trying to catch a snake. If you grab the snake by its body, it can turn around and bite you. But if you know how to catch it by pinning it down behind its head with a forked stick, it will not harm anyone. "If you do not bring your whole heart, mind, and being into listening to the Dharma, you may understand it incorrectly, and it will bring more harm than good to you and others. Studying the Dharma, you must be careful and attentive."

The Buddha also said, "There are always some people who study the sutras only to satisfy their curiosity or win arguments, and not for the sake of liberation. With such a motivation, they miss the true spirit of the teaching. They may go through hardship, endure difficulties that are not of much benefit, and exhaust themselves.

"Bhikkhus, a person who studies that way can be compared to a man trying to catch a poisonous snake in the wild. If he reaches out his hand, the snake may bite his hand, leg, or some other part of his body. Trying to catch a snake that way has no advantages and can only create suffering.

"Bhikkhus, understanding my teaching in the wrong way is the same. If you do not practice the Dharma correctly, you may come to understand it as the opposite of what was intended. But if you practice intelligently, you will understand both the letter and the spirit of the teachings and will be able to explain them correctly. Do not practice just to show off or argue with others. Practice to attain liberation, and if you do, you will have little pain or exhaustion.

"Bhikkhus, an intelligent student of the Dharma is like a man who uses a forked stick to catch a snake. When he sees a poisonous snake in the wild, he places the stick right below the head of the snake and grabs the snake's neck with his hand. Even if the snake winds itself around the man's hand, leg, or another part of his body, it will not bite him. This is the better way to catch a snake, and it will not lead to pain or exhaustion."

When we look deeply at this early Buddhist sutra, we can see many methods proposed to us later in the Mahayana sutras. The *Prajñaparamita Diamond Sutra* has a sentence that is almost word-for-word from this sutra: "Even the Dharma has to be abandoned, not to mention the non-Dharma." Even if it is the true Dharma, you still have to let it go and not cling too tightly.

Throughout the *Tripitaka*, the Buddhist canon, there are examples of misunderstandings of the Buddha's teachings. One time, before going on a personal retreat near the city of Vaisali, the Buddha gave a Dharma talk about impermanence, impurity of the body, and non-self. Some monks misunderstood him and said, "This life is not worth living. Everything is impure and must be abandoned. Then, after the Buddha left for his retreat, several of them committed suicide right in the monastery where the Buddha had spoken.

How could monks misunderstand the Buddha so? How could they think this to be the true teaching of the Buddha? In fact, there are people in our day who still think this way. The Buddha taught that suffering exists, so they think that in order to stop suffering, they have to stop existence. It is easy to misunderstand the teaching of the Buddha. The monk Yamaka propagated that idea until one day, Shariputra became aware of it and gave him proper instruction.

In the *Sutra on Knowing the Better Way to Catch a Snake*, a monk named Arittha said that the Buddha taught that sense pleasures are not an obstacle to the practice. His fellow monks tried to dissuade him from saying that, but he continued to hold this view. Hearing that, the Buddha summoned Arittha and, in the presence of many monks, asked, "Arittha, is it true you have been saying that I teach that sense pleasures are not an obstacle to the practice?"

Arittha replied, "Yes, Lord, I do believe that according to the spirit of your teachings, sense pleasures are not an obstacle to the practice."

I spent a lot of time reflecting on this passage, and I also did some research. When you read any sutra, you should keep in mind the context of the sutra as well as the whole teaching of the Buddha, so you can understand what really happened. I discovered that Arittha was an intelligent monk with a very appealing personality who had heard the Buddha speak about the practice of self-mortification, sharing his own experience of six years practicing asceticism. The Buddha discovered that asceticism is not helpful—to get enlightened, you have to take care of your body—so he accepted rice milk and other offerings of food from the villagers of Uruvela.

The Buddha was a happy person, quite capable of enjoying a beautiful morning or a glass of clear water. One time, standing on Vulture Peak with Ananda, he pointed to the rice fields below and said, "Ananda, aren't these fields beautiful when the rice is ripe? Let us design the robes of the monks in this pattern." Another time, when passing by the town of Vaisali, he said, "Ananda, how beautiful Vaisali is." When King Mahanama invited the Buddha and his monks for a meal, the Buddha made this remark, "Mahanama offered us the best kind of food." The Buddha was well aware of the quality of the food.

I have met monks who do not dare say that the food they eat is tasty. One day in Thailand, I was offered delicious sweet rice and mango. I enjoyed it very much, and I told my hosts, "This is so good." I was aware that Thai monks do not say that, but I think it is safe to enjoy what is around you and within you as long as you are aware of its nature of impermanence. When you are thirsty, there is nothing wrong in enjoying a glass of water. In fact, to truly enjoy it, you have to dwell in the present moment.

When a flower dies, we don't cry. We know it is impermanent. If we practice awareness of the nature of impermanence, we will suffer less and enjoy life more. If we know things are impermanent, we will cherish them in the present moment. We know that our loved ones are of impermanent nature, so we try our best to make them happy now. Impermanence is not negative. Some Buddhists think we should not enjoy anything, because everything is impermanent. They think that emancipation is to get rid of everything and not enjoy anything. But when we offer flowers to the Buddha, I believe the Buddha sees the beauty of the flowers and deeply appreciates them. It seems that Arittha was unable to distinguish between enjoying the well-being of body and mind, and indulging in sensual pleasures.

In the *Vimalakirti Sutra*, the silence of the layman Vimalakirti is praised by the Bodhisattva Manjushri as a "thundering silence" that echoes far and wide, having the power to break the bonds of attachment and bring about liberation. It is the same as the lion's roar that proclaims, "It is necessary to let go of all the true teachings, not to mention teachings that are not true." This is the spirit we need if we want to understand the *Sutra on Knowing the Better Way to Catch a Snake.*

In the *Snake Sutra*, the Buddha also tells us that the Dharma is a raft we can use to cross the river and get to the other shore. But after we have crossed the river, if we continue to carry the raft on our shoulders, that would be foolish. "The raft is not the shore." These are the Buddha's words: "Bhikkhus, I have told you many times the importance of knowing when it is time to let go of a raft and not hold onto it unnecessarily. When a mountain stream overflows and becomes a torrent of floodwater carrying debris, a man or woman who wants to get across might think, What is the safest way to cross this floodwater? Assessing the situation, she may decide to gather branches and grasses, construct a raft, and use it to cross to the other side. But, after arriving on the other side, she thinks, I spent a lot of time and energy building this raft. It is a prized possession, and I will carry it with me as I continue my journey. If she puts it on her shoulders or head and carries it with her on land, Bhikkhus, do you think that would be intelligent?"

The Bhikkhus replied, "No, World-Honored One."

The Buddha said, "How could she have acted more wisely? She could have thought, This raft helped me get across the water safely. Now I will leave it at the water's edge for someone else to use in the same way. Wouldn't that be a more intelligent thing to do?"

The Bhikkhus replied, "Yes, World-Honored One."

The Buddha taught, "I have given this teaching on the raft many times to remind you how necessary it is to let go of all the true teachings, not to mention teachings that are not true."

The first aspect of Buddhist meditation is *samatha* (stopping and calming), and the second is *vipasyana* (insight, looking deeply). There is a branch of early Buddhism that has become known as *vipassana* (the Pali equivalent of the Sanskrit "vipasyana"). If we study Mahayana Buddhism, we will see that vipasyana, looking deeply, is very much at its heart. Many concrete practices are offered by the Buddha to help the bodhisattvas obtain insight and achieve transformation, not just for themselves but for all beings.

When we study the *Sutra on Knowing the Better Way to catch a Snake*, an early teaching of the Buddha, we recognize it as an excellent introduction to the teachings of Mahayana Buddhism. Its attitude of openness, non-attachment from views, and playfulness serves well as a Dharma door to enter the realm of Mahayana Buddhism, helping us see clearly that all the seeds of Mahayana thought and practice were already present in the early teachings of the Buddha.

SIX

The Guard

It was more difficult for her than it was for me. She had faith and confidence in me as a big brother, and I felt a real sense of responsibility toward her. On the day the abbot was expected to return, she was very calm and quiet. She spoke and walked exactly as before, but her smile was more radiant. When you are loved, you emit a great confidence.

That day, the last day of the lunar year, we had tea and a Dharma discussion for many hours. We belonged to the first generation of monks and nuns in Vietnam who had received a Western education. More than anything we wanted to help the people of our country during the time of war. But the teachings offered by the Buddhist institutes had not changed for centuries. We were motivated by the desire to bring peace, reconciliation, and brotherhood to our society, and we felt frustrated that our teachers never addressed these needs. Every tradition has to renew itself from time to time in order to address the pressing issues of the day and offer the kinds of practices that are needed to renew itself.

I lived and practiced with five other young monks in a small Buddhist temple in the outskirts of Saigon. We had left the Buddhist Institute in Huê because we felt we were not getting the teachings we needed. In Saigon, I edited a Buddhist magazine, and our community used the stipend from that to support itself. We six monks also attended school, studying among other subjects Western philosophy and science, because we were convinced that these subjects could help us infuse life into the practice of Buddhism in our country. You have to speak the language of your time to express the Buddha's teachings in ways people can understand.

It was clear from our Dharma discussions that we shared the same ideals. She had already proposed to one sister that they form a center for young nuns to practice in much the same way that we six monks were practicing. I told her about a temple not far from ours that might be available. I was not aware that my suggestion was, in part, motivated by the desire to see her again.

By three o'clock in the afternoon, the abbot had still not arrived, so we continued our discussion. I said that in the future I wanted to see monks and nuns operating high schools, taking care of kindergartens, and running health-care centers, practicing meditation while doing the work of helping people—not just talking about compassion, but expressing compassion through action. Since then, this has all become a reality. Monks and nuns in Vietnam now help prostitutes, teach street children, and do many other kinds of social work. But at that time, these projects were just a dream. As we discussed these things, I could see her happiness, so I continued to talk until my throat became sore. Seeing that, she went to her room and brought me some cough drops. I still remember the trademark on the box, *Pâtes des Vosges*. If the abbot had given me that box of cough drops, I don't think I would still remember the name.

After dinner, we practiced sitting and chanting, and then we went to our rooms. Neither of us had slept much for three days, and we knew we needed to sleep well to regain our health and be presentable for the abbot, who would surely return the next day. But it was impossible to sleep. At one o'clock, I was still awake, and I felt a strong desire to be with her—to sit with her, to look at her, to listen to her. I knew it would be the last time we would have some privacy. During many moments that night, I felt the desire to go and knock on her door and invite her to the sitting hall to continue our discussion. But I did not, because we had an agreement, and I had to honor that. I had the impression she was probably awake and that if I went to her room and knocked, she would be happy to go to the hall to continue our conversation. But I resisted. Something very strong in me protected her, and me.

During that night and all the previous days and nights, I never even had the idea to hold her hands in mine or to kiss her on the forehead. She represented everything I loved—my ideal of compassion, loving kindness, bringing Buddhism into society, and realizing peace and reconciliation. That desire in me was so strong and sacred that anything like holding her hand or kissing her on the forehead would have been a violation. She represented all that was important in my life, and I could not afford to shatter it.

She was in her room like a princess, and the bodhichitta in me was the guard, protecting her. I knew that if anything happened to her, we would both lose everything—the Buddha, our ideal of compassion, and the desire to actualize Buddhism. I did not have to make any effort to practice the precepts. Our strong desire to realize the Dharma protected us both. For our lives to continue, I could not be less than a monk nor she less than a nun. As commander of the troops guarding her, it was impossible for me to open the door, walk to her room, and knock at her door. That would have destroyed everything.

SEVEN

The Diamond
That Cuts through Illusion

A diamond can cut everything, but nothing can cut a diamond. We need to develop diamond-like insight to cut through our afflictions. If you study the *Sutra on Knowing the Better Way to Catch a Snake* and then the *Diamond Sutra*, you will see the connection between these two scriptures.

The *Diamond Sutra* records a conversation between the Buddha and his disciple Subhuti. It is one of the earliest *Prajñaparamita Sutras*. One thousand two hundred fifty bhikshus are present. In later *Prajñaparamita Sutras*, there are few bhikshus and many bodhisattvas—25,000 or 50,000. The question put forth by Subhuti is, "World-Honored One, if sons and daughters of good families want to give rise to the highest, most fulfilled, awakened mind, what should they rely on and what should they do to master their thinking?" Subhuti was aware that the beginning of the bodhisattva career is bodhichitta, the desire to bring ourselves and other living beings to the shore of happiness and freedom.

This is the Buddha's answer: "However many species of living beings there are—whether born from eggs, from the womb, from moisture, or spontaneously; whether they have form or do not have form; whether they have perceptions or do not have perceptions; or whether it cannot be said of them that they have perceptions or that they do not have perceptions, we must lead all these beings to the ultimate nirvana so that they can be liberated." We have to vow to practice for everyone, not just for ourselves. We practice for the trees, the animals, the rocks, and the water. We practice for living beings with form and living beings without form, for living beings with perceptions and living beings without perceptions. We vow to bring all these beings to the shore of liberation. And yet, when we have brought all of them to the shore of liberation, we realize that no being at all has been brought to the shore of liberation. This is the spirit of Mahayana Buddhism.

There are forty verses summarizing the teaching of the *Prajñaparamita Diamond Sutra*. Every Buddhist who practices insight, vipasyana, has prajñaparamita, perfect understanding, as his or her mother. Living beings have never been born and are pure from the very start. That is the practice of the highest perfection. The bodhisattva, while carrying living beings to the other shore, does not see a single being. This is not difficult to understand. Just relax and allow the Dharma rain to come in. I am sure you will understand.

According to the Lord Buddha, there are four notions we have to examine carefully: self, person, living being, and life span. "When this innumerable, immeasurable, infinite number of beings has become liberated, we do not, in truth, think that a single being has been liberated. Why is this so? If, Subhuti, a bodhisattva holds on to the idea that a self, a person, a living being, or a life span exists, that person is not an authentic bodhisattva." The bodhisattva is one who is liberated from the notions of self, person, living being, and life span.

We know that a flower is made only of non-flower elements, like sunshine, earth, water, time, and space. Everything in the cosmos comes together to bring about the presence of one flower, and these boundless conditions are what we call "non-flower elements." Compost helps make the flower, and the flower creates more compost. If we meditate, we can see the compost right here and now in the flower. If you are an organic gardener, you know that already.

These are not just words. It is our experience, the fruit of our practice of looking deeply. Looking at anything, we can see the nature of interbeing. A self is not possible without non-self elements. Looking deeply at any one thing, we see the whole cosmos. The one is made of the many. To take care of ourselves, we take care of those around us. Their happiness and stability are our happiness and stability. If we are free of the notions of self and non-self, we will not be afraid of the words self and non-self. But if we see the self as our enemy and think that non-self is our savior, we are caught. We are trying to push away one thing and embrace another. When we realize that to take care of the self is to take care of non-self, we are free, and we don't have to push away either.

The Buddha said, "Take refuge in the island of self." He was not afraid to use the word "self," because he was free of notions. But we students of the Buddha do not dare use the word. Several years ago, when I proposed a gatha for listening to the bell, "Listen, listen. This wonderful sound brings me back to my true self," a number of Buddhists refused to recite it because it included the word "self." So they changed it to, "Listen, listen. This wonderful sound brings me back to my true nature." They tried to escape "self" in order to be serious students of the Buddha, but instead they just became prisoners of their notions.

If a bodhisattva holds on to the idea that a self, a person, a living being, or a life span exists, that person is not an authentic bodhisattva. If we are aware that the self is always made of non-self elements, we will never be enslaved by or afraid of the notion of self or non-self. If we say the notion of self is harmful or dangerous, the notion of non-self may be even more dangerous. Clinging to the notion of self is not good, but clinging to the notion of non-self is worse.

Understanding that self is made only of non-self elements is safe. The Buddha did not say, "You don't exist." He only said, "You are without self." Your nature is non-self. We suffer, because we think he said we don't exist. From one extreme we fall into another extreme, but both extremes are just our notions. We never experience reality. We only have these notions, and we suffer because of them.

We have a notion of person as distinguished from non-person, such as a tree, a deer, a squirrel, a hawk, air, or water. But "person" is also a notion to be transcended. It is made only of non-person elements. If you believe that God made man first and after that he created trees, fruits, water, and sky, you are not in agreement with the *Diamond Sutra*. The *Diamond Sutra* teaches that man is made of non-man elements. Without trees, man cannot be. Without fruits, water, and sky, man cannot be.

This is the practice of looking deeply, touching reality, and living in mindfulness. You look at and touch everything as an experience, not as a notion. The notion of man as more important than other species is a wrong notion. The Buddha taught us to take good care of our environment. He knew that if we take care of the trees, we take care of man. We must live our daily lives with that kind of awareness. This is not philosophy. We desperately need mindfulness for our children and their children to be safe. The idea that man can do everything he wants at the expense of so-called non-man elements is an ignorant and dangerous notion.

Breathe in with the deep awareness that you are a human being. Then breathe out and touch the Earth, a non-man element, as your mother. Visualize the streams of water beneath the Earth's surface. See the minerals. See our Mother Earth, the mother of us all. Then bring your arms up and breathe in again, touching the trees, flowers, fruits, birds, squirrels, air and sky—the non-man elements. When your head is touching the air, the sun, the moon, the galaxies, the cosmos—non-man elements that have come together in order to make man possible—you see that all of the elements are coming into you to make your being possible. Breathing in again, stretch your arms and be aware that you also penetrate other elements. Man helps make the other elements possible.

Let us look together at the notion "living being." Living beings are beings that have sensations. Non-living beings are beings that have no sensations. Actually, scientists find it difficult to establish the boundary. Some are not certain whether mushrooms are animals or plants. The French poet Lamartine asked whether inanimate objects have a soul. I would say yes. The Vietnamese composer Trinh Cong Son said, "Tomorrow even rocks and pebbles will need each other." How do we know that rocks do not suffer? After the atomic bomb fell on Hiroshima, the rocks in the parks there were dead, and the Japanese carried them away and brought in living rocks.

In Mahayana Buddhist temples, we make the vow that every being, animate or inanimate, will realize full and perfect enlightenment. Although we use the words animate and inanimate, we are aware that all are beings, and that the distinction between living and non-living beings is spurious. A true bodhisattva can see that living beings are made of non-living elements. The notion "living beings" is dissolved, and the bodhisattva is emancipated. A bodhisattva devotes his or her life to helping bring living beings "to the other shore," without clinging to the notion "living beings."

Because of our tendency to use notions and concepts to grasp reality, we cannot touch reality as it is. We construct an image of reality that does not coincide with reality itself. That is why these exercises are important to help us free ourselves. They are not philosophical. If we try to make the Buddha's teaching into a doctrine, we miss the point. We have caught the snake by its tail. During our daily lives, we practice living mindfully in order to get in touch with reality, and we observe things in order to see the true nature of non-self. Many people misunderstand this teaching of the Buddha. They think that he is denying the existence of living beings. It is not a denial. The Buddha is offering us an instrument to help us reach a deeper understanding and emancipation. The instrument should be used, not worshipped. The raft is not the shore.

The first three notions—self, person, and living being—are presented in terms of space. The fourth notion—life span—is presented in terms of time. Before you were born, did you exist? Was there a self? When did you begin to have a self? From the moment of conception? The sword of discrimination cuts reality into two pieces—the period of your nonexistence and the period when you began to exist. How will you continue? After you die, will you become nothing again? This is a frightening notion that all humans ponder. What will happen after I die? When we hear, "There is no self," we become even more frightened. It is comforting to say, "I exist," so we ask, "What happens after I die?" We attempt to hold onto a notion of self that makes us feel comfortable. "This is the world. This is the self. I will continue."

The Buddha made a simple statement concerning the existence of things: "This is, because that is. This is not, because that is not." Everything relies upon everything else in order to be. We need to understand what the Buddha meant by "to be." Our notion of being might be different from his. We cannot say that the Buddha confirmed "being" and denied "non-being." That would be like catching a snake by its tail. When he said, "This is, because that is," the Buddha was not trying to establish a theory of being that denies non-being. That is the opposite of what he meant.

In Western philosophy, the term "being-in-itself" is very close to the Buddhist term "suchness," reality as it is, free from conceptions or grasping. You cannot grasp it, because grasping reality with concepts and notions is like catching space with a net. The technique, therefore, is to stop using concepts and notions and enter reality in a non-conceptual instant. The Buddha handed us an instrument to remove notions and concepts and touch reality directly. If you continue to cling even to Buddhist notions and concepts, you miss the opportunity. You are carrying the raft on your shoulders. Do not be a prisoner of any doctrine or ideology, even Buddhist ones.

The mode of being expressed by the Buddha is at the heart of reality. It is not the notion we usually construct for ourselves. Our notion of being is dualistic, the opposite of the notion of non-being. The reality of being the

Buddha tries to convey is not the opposite of non-being. He is using language differently. When he says "self," it is not the opposite of anything. The Buddha is very aware that self is made of non-self elements. That is our true self.

Is it possible to abandon our notions of being and non-being in order to touch true being? Of course. Otherwise, what is the use of practicing? In Mahayana Buddhism, we use anti-notions to help us get rid of notions. If you get caught by the notion of being, the notion of emptiness is there to rescue you. But if you forget that true emptiness is filled with everything, you will be caught by your notion of emptiness and bitten by the snake. *The Ratnakuta Sutra* says it is better to be caught by the notion of being than by the notion of emptiness. All other notions can be healed by the notion of emptiness, but when you are caught in the notion of emptiness, the disease is incurable.

The belief that the self is there before I was born and will continue after I die is a belief in permanence. The opposite belief—that after you die you enter into absolute nothingness—is a belief in annihilation. These kinds of wrong views are discussed in the *Sutra on Knowing the Better Way to Catch a Snake*. Buddhist practitioners must take care not to fall into either trap—the belief in a permanent self (whether great or small) or the belief in annihilation (becoming nothing). These two notions must be transcended. Many Buddhists are not capable of doing so, and they are caught in one notion or the other, getting bitten by the snake over and over again.

One day, I was contemplating a stick of burning incense. The smoke coming off its tip was creating many beautiful forms in the air. It seemed alive, really there. I perceived an existence, a being, a life, and I sat quietly enjoying myself and the "self" of the incense stick. I enjoyed the smoke as it continued to drift up creating various forms. I used my left hand to "catch" the smoke. The last moment the stick was burning was especially beautiful. When there was no more incense at the other end, there was more oxygen on both sides, so it burned most intensely for a moment, revealing a bright red color. I looked at it with all my concentration. It was a parinirvana, a great extinction. Where had the flame gone?

When a person is about to die, he or she often becomes very alert at that last moment of life and then fades away, just like the stick of incense. Where has the soul gone? I had several other sticks of incense, and I knew that if, at that last moment, I took another stick of incense and touched the first stick with it, the flame would have continued onto the new stick, and the life of the incense would have continued. It was only a matter of fuel, or conditions.

The teaching of the Buddha is very clear: when certain conditions are present, our senses perceive something and we qualify it as "being." When those conditions are no longer sufficient, our senses perceive the absence of that something, and we qualify it as "non-being." That is a wrong perception. The box of incense has many sticks. If

I feed one stick after another to the fuel, is the life of the incense eternal?

Is the Buddha alive or dead? It is a matter of fuel. Perhaps you are the fuel, and you continue the life of the Buddha. We cannot say the Buddha is alive or dead. Reality transcends birth, death, production, and destruction. "What was your face before your parents were born?" This is an invitation to find your true self that is not subject to birth and death.

EIGHT

Saying Good-bye

On New Year's morning, after sitting and chanting to-gether, we heard the people from the village come into the temple, bringing fruit, flowers, and all that was needed to celebrate Têt. I helped them decorate the Buddha Hall and she helped in the kitchen. Then, the abbot arrived. No one seemed to know what had happened, not even the young lady who had prepared our meals. On the second day of the New Year, I left to return to my temple. I had little hope of seeing her again.

I came home a different person, but my brothers in the Dharma did not notice. My daily life must have looked almost normal, even though I was talking less and spend-ing more time alone. At times, I just called her name in a soft voice to keep from missing her too much. All I could do was continue my studies and practice.

Then one day, when I came home, she was there. She had succeeded in carrying out the proposal I'd made. She and another nun had moved into the abandoned temple near ours to set up a small center where nuns could study, practice, and engage in social work. We six monks were very happy to have Dharma sisters who shared our ideals and aspirations living so close. I proposed that they join us in Buddhist studies.

To help her Dharma sister improve her Chinese, I asked her to translate into Vietnamese a book written by a Chinese scientist who had studied Buddhism. I checked the translation and corrected many passages. She did not understand well the Chinese original. As for her, to help her improve her French, I gave her a book on Buddhism in French to translate. Doing that would improve their Chinese, their French, and their understanding of Buddhism. But every time I gave her a lesson, we stayed together longer than was necessary. In two or three weeks, my brothers in the Dharma saw this and realized I was in love (it would have been difficult not to notice), and to my great surprise, they accepted it without criticism. The feeling of gratitude for their acceptance is still in my heart.

But when her Dharma sister found out, she could not accept it. One day, I saw a tear in her eye, and I understood. I knew I had to solve the problem.

The next day, after our lesson, I said, "Dear younger sister, I think you should go to Van Ho, a new Buddhist Institute in Hanoi. We will continue to study, practice, and search. Someday, we will find it." That Buddhist Institute was run by a nun with a very open outlook. I hoped that from there she would be able to motivate other sisters to help bring about the kinds of changes we had discussed. It was a difficult decision because she would be at the other end of the country, but I felt I had no choice.

She bowed her head and said only one word, "Yes." She had complete faith and trust in me. How could I not feel responsible?

I was overwhelmed by sadness. In me, there was the element of attachment, but there was also the voice of wisdom recognizing that for us to continue to be ourselves, to succeed in our attempt to search and to realize, this was the only way.

I remember the moment we parted. We sat across from each other. She, too, seemed overwhelmed by despair. She stood up, came close to me, took my head in her arms, and drew me close to her in a very natural way. I allowed myself to be embraced. It was the first and last time we had any physical contact. Then we bowed and separated.

NINE

Three Dharma Seals

Every authentic teaching of the Buddha must bear Three Dharma Seals: impermanence, non-self, and nirvana. The first Dharma Seal is impermanence. Nothing remains the same for two consecutive moments. Heraclitus said we can never bathe twice in the same river. Confucius, while looking at a stream, said, "It is always flowing, day and night." The Buddha implored us not just to talk about impermanence, but to use it as an instrument to help us penetrate deeply into reality and obtain liberating insight.

We may be tempted to say that because things are impermanent, there is suffering. But the Buddha encouraged us to look again. Without impermanence, life is not possible. How can we transform our suffering if things are not impermanent? How can our daughter grow up into a beautiful young lady? How can the situation in the world improve? We need impermanence for social justice and for hope.

If you suffer, it is not because things are impermanent. It is because you believe things are permanent. When a flower dies, you don't suffer much, because you understand that flowers are impermanent. But you cannot accept the impermanence of your beloved one, and you suffer deeply when she passes away. If you look deeply into impermanence, you will do your best to make her happy right now. Aware of impermanence, you become positive, loving, and wise. Impermanence is good news. Without impermanence, nothing would be possible. With impermanence, every door is open for change. Instead of complaining, we should say, "Long live impermanence!" Impermanence is an instrument for our liberation.

The second Dharma Seal is non-self. If you believe in a permanent self, a self that exists forever, a separate, independent self, your belief cannot be described as Buddhist. Impermanence is from the point of view of time; non-self is from the point of view of space.

When we practice the *Diamond Sutra* and look more and more deeply at the notions of self, person, living being, and life span, we discover that there are no boundaries between self and non-self, person and non-person, living being and non-living being, life span and non-life span. When we take a step on the green earth, we are aware that we are made of air, sunshine, minerals, and water, that we are a child of earth and sky, linked to all other beings, both animate and inanimate. This is the practice of non-self. The Buddha invites us to dwell in mindfulness in the concentrations (*samadhi*) of interbeing, non-self, and impermanence.

The third Dharma Seal is nirvana, which means "extinction," the extinction of afflictions and notions. Human beings' three basic afflictions are craving, hatred, and ignorance. Ignorance (*avidya*), the inability to understand reality, is the most fundamental of these. Because we are ignorant, we crave for things that destroy us, and we get angry at many things. We try to grasp the world of our projections, and we suffer. Nirvana, the extinction of all afflictions, represents the birth of freedom. The extinction of one thing always brings about the birth of something else. When darkness is extinguished, light comes forth. When suffering is removed, peace and happiness are always there.

Many scholars say that nirvana is annihilation, the extinction of everything, and that Buddhists aspire to nonbeing. They have been bitten by the snake of nirvana. In many sutras, the Buddha says that although ascetics and brahmans describe his teaching as annihilation and nonbeing, that is not correct. The Buddha offers us nirvana to rescue us from attachment to the notions of impermanence and non-self. If we get caught by nirvana, how will we ever escape?

Notions and concepts can be useful if we learn how to use them skillfully, without getting caught by them. Zen master Lin Chi said, "If you see the Buddha on your way, kill him." He means if you have an idea of the Buddha that prevents you from having a direct experience of the Buddha, you are caught by that object of your perception, and the only way for you to free yourself and experience the Buddha is to kill your notion of the Buddha. This is the secret of the practice. If you hold onto an idea or a notion, you lose the chance. Learning to transcend your mental constructions of reality is an art. Teachers have to help their students learn how not to accumulate notions. If you are laden with notions, you will never be emancipated. Learning to look deeply to see into the true nature of things, having direct contact with reality and not just describing reality in terms of notions and concepts, is the practice.

Every teaching that bears the mark of the Three Dharma Seals is truly the Buddhadharma. The Buddha offers us impermanence as an instrument for looking deeply, but if we get caught by impermanence, he offers us the instrument of non-self. If we get caught again, he offers us nirvana, the extinction of afflictions and notions. In the *Hundred Parables Sutra*, the Buddha tells the story of a man who is thirsty. When people tell him to go to the river, he sees so much water that he becomes bewildered and asks, "How can I drink all this water?" He refuses to drink and dies on the riverbank. Many of us die the same way. If we embrace the Buddha's Dharma as a notion, we will die of suffering born from misunderstanding of the true nature of things. But if we practice the Buddhadharma, applying our own intelligence, we have a chance to drink the water and cross the river to the other shore.

TEN

Swimming Upstream

Two months after she left for Hanoi, I received a letter saying that she had followed my instructions exactly and that although it was difficult for her, things were working out. I wrote back confirming my love and support. It was a difficult time for both of us, but our separation also had many positive effects. With time and distance, we were able to grow, to see things differently, and our love became more mature. The element of attachment had lessened, allowing compassion and loving kindness to flower. Separation did not destroy our love. It strengthened it.

I want you to know that, to me, there is no difference between the *Snake Sutra*, the *Diamond Sutra*, and this love story. Hearing the love story can help you understand the Dharma, and hearing the Dharma can help you understand the love story. You may ask, "What happened next?" What happened next is up to you. If you ask, "What is her name? Where is she now?", you might as well ask, "Who is Thây? What has happened to him?" This story is happening to you and to me right now. With an open heart, through the practice of looking deeply, we have a chance to touch the reality. This is the way taught by the *Diamond Sutra*.

The expression "first love" is misleading, so I went "upstream" to tell you other stories—seeing the Buddha on the cover of a magazine, drinking from the clear well, my brother becoming a monk. If the drawing had not been there, if the well had not been there, if my brother had not become a monk, how could I have seen her? She is made of the "non-she" elements that came from the stream of my life, from even before I was born. My ancestors had already met her. My "first" love has always been there. She has no beginning. The moment I understood that, she became transformed into something much more powerful. That seed of deep love is in every one of us.

Drinking the water on the hermit's mountain, the stream of fresh water in my own river was nourished. Seeing the drawing of the Buddha was also part of the stream flowing into my river. So were my mother and big brother. In fact, these streams are still entering my river. I am made only of "non-me" elements—the hermit, the Buddha, my mother, my brother, and her. If you ask, "What happened next?", you are forgetting that the self is made of non-self elements. Because you are there, I am here. What happens next depends on you.

In 1954, the Geneva Accords were signed, dividing Vietnam into north and south, and she left Hanoi and returned to her original Buddhist Institute in Huê. I was glad, because she would be in the same part of the country as I was, south of the seventeenth parallel, and there would be opportunities for us to see each other again. I wrote to her, as always offering my full support. Many refugees—Buddhists and Catholics—migrated from north to south. It was a time of great confusion in the country. I had written several popular books about engaged Buddhism, and in 1954 a daily newspaper asked me to write a series of articles on Buddhism to help people deal with these real problems. The articles were printed on the front page with large headlines, such as "Buddhism and the Question of God" and "Buddhism and the Problems of Democracy," presenting Buddhism as something very refreshing and relevant.

It was also a time of uncertainty among the Buddhist establishment, and I was invited by the An Quang Buddhist Institute, one of the most prestigious institutions of Buddhist learning in southern Vietnam, to propose a new curriculum. We young monks and nuns wanted to practice a kind of Buddhism that is alive, that could address our deepest needs, that could help bring peace, reconciliation, and well-being to our country. Being asked by the board of the Institute to develop a new teaching program was a great opportunity to realize our dream. So I convened a series of meetings involving hundreds of young monks, nuns, and others, and we created an atmosphere of hope, trust, and love. The Patriarch of the Unified Buddhist Church joined one of our meetings, and he listened as we young monks and nuns expressed our deepest hopes for Buddhism in our country.

When I spoke about the way to bring Buddhism into society and the kind of practice I thought we needed, many people cried. For the first time, we began to see the future.

We proposed that the An Quang Buddhist Institute curriculum include not only the basic teachings of Buddhism, but also Western philosophy, languages, science, and other subjects that could help us understand our society and the contemporary world. It was exhilarating to be involved in what I had dreamed about for such a long time. Of course, there was resistance from the conservative Buddhist hierarchy and from laypeople who were not ready to accept the changes, but supported by young monks, young nuns, and young lay Buddhists, our proposals were eventually accepted. We began publishing a magazine called *The First Lotus Flowers of the Season*, thinking of the young monks and nuns who were the new lotuses for our time. In that magazine, we expressed ourselves naturally and in modern ways. I supported the young monks and nuns, because I knew the difficulties and suffering they encountered. Many of these same monks and nuns are now teaching in Vietnam and in the West. But she was not there. She was in Huê. I wrote many letters to inform her of all these events, to support her, and to show my love, but I received no response.

In 1956, I flew to Huê. By that time I was well-known in the country as a Buddhist teacher and writer who cared for the younger generation. I went first to visit my first teacher, whom I had not seen for a long time, and I spent two wonderful weeks at my home temple with him. Then I went to see my family, and after that I spent several weeks at the Buddhist Institute where I had first studied and practiced. I felt welcome everywhere.

I had written to her saying that I was coming, and I assumed she would ask permission to accompany a Dharma sister to visit me at my temple. That would have been natural. It would not have been proper for me to just go to her Institute and ask to see her. But she did not come to see me at all, and I couldn't understand why. Later I learned that she had never received my letters and didn't even know I was there.

My love for her did not diminish, but it was no longer confined to one person. I was supporting hundreds of monks and nuns, and since that time we have become thousands, yet that love is still here, stronger and larger. In 1956, there were almost no monks and nuns in Vietnam practicing social service. Today many are doctors, nurses, teachers, day-care workers, and so on, practicing compassion and loving kindness every day. At Plum Village, we are also part of that practice. Engaged Buddhism has become widespread, even in the West. But then it was all new, and I had to devote myself to writing books and practicing well to help bring about the actualization of Buddhism.

If you want to know what happened next, please look deep within yourself. What happened next continues today. When you are serene—smiling, breathing in and out mindfully—I know that you understand. But when you are stuck in the notion of a self, a person, a living being, or a life span, you cannot understand the nature of my true love, which is reverence, trust, and faith. The best way to support our love is to be truly yourself, to grow, and to cultivate deep self-respect. With your contentment, you support us all, including her and including me. Somehow she is still here.

Please look into the river of your own life, and see the many streams that have entered it, that nourish and support you. If you practice the *Diamond Sutra* and see the self beyond the self, the person beyond the person, the living being beyond the living being, the life span beyond the life span, you will see that you are me, and you are also her. Look back at your own first love and you will recognize that your first love has no beginning and no end. It is always in transformation.

ELEVEN

Doors of Liberation

The Three Doors of Liberation—emptiness, signlessness, and wishlessness—are common to all schools of Buddhism. The first is emptiness, *sunyata*.

Empty always means empty of something, so we must ask, "Empty of what?" If I drink all the water in a glass, the glass is empty of water, but it is not empty of air. Emptiness *does not* mean nonexistent. If Avalokiteshvara tells us that the five *skandhas* are empty, we have to ask, "Empty of what?" If we do, he will tell us, "Empty of a separate existence." It means "A" is made entirely of "non-A" elements. This sheet of paper is empty of a separate existence, because it cannot exist by itself; it has to *inter-be* with every other thing. Our sheet of paper is made of non-paper elements, like trees, sunshine, rain, soil, minerals, time, space, and consciousness. It is empty of a separate self, but it is full of everything else. So emptiness means fullness at the same time. The teachings of interbeing and interdependence can be touched. Emptiness is a Door of Liberation, a practice, not just a subject for discussion. Look deeply at everything, and you will find the true nature of emptiness. When you do, you will remove discrimination and transcend the fear of birth and death.

The second Door of Liberation is signlessness, *alakshana*. Can we recognize the Buddha through signs? If we are caught by signs, we lose the Buddha. The *Diamond Sutra* tells us, "In a place where something can be distinguished by signs, in that place there is deception." Deception is born from signs, and so our practice is to transcend signs. If we get stuck in a notion or a sign, this Door of Liberation will close. We must open the door using the key of signlessness. Don't try to grasp reality through signs. Don't believe in your perceptions too much.

In the *Diamond Sutra*, the Buddha asks, "What do you think, Subhuti? Is it possible to grasp the Tathagata by means of bodily signs?" And Subhuti replies, "No, World-Honored One. When the Tathagata speaks of bodily signs, there are no signs being talked about." Subhuti is using the language of prajñaparamita. That is why he says, "When the Tathagata speaks of bodily signs, there are no signs being talked about." If you can see the signless nature of signs, you can see the Tathagata. How can we find the Tathagata? The Buddha tells us that we cannot grasp him by our notions. The word "sign" is used here. We can also use the words "mark," "external appearance," "phenomenon," or "designation" (*lakshana* or *nimitta*). A sign or a mark is never the reality itself.

Because of our ignorance and habit-energies, we usually perceive things incorrectly. We are caught in our mental categories, especially our notions of self, person, living being, and life span. We discriminate between self and non-self, as if self has nothing to do with non-self. We take care of the well-being of the self, but we do not think much about the well-being of everything that is non-self. When we see things this way, our behavior will be based on wrong perceptions. Our mind is like a sword cutting reality into pieces, and then we act as though each piece of reality is independent from the other pieces. If we look deeply, we will remove these barriers between our mental categories and see the one in the many and the many in the one, which is the true nature of interbeing. This is the way to be free from our notions. That is why in the *Diamond Sutra*, the Buddha uses the language of freedom when he responds to his disciple Subhuti. We see many sentences like this in the *Diamond Sutra*: "A bodhisattva is not a bodhisattva, that is why he is truly a bodhisattva." This way of talking is called the dialectics of prajñaparamita. It is offered by the Buddha to free us from notions.

Let us try to understand the dialectics of prajñaparamita: A cup is not a cup, therefore it is truly a cup. A self is not a self, that is why it can be truly a self. When we look into "A," the thing we are observing—a cup, a self, a mountain, a government—we see the "non-A" elements in it. In fact, "A" is made only of "non-A" elements, so we can say that "A" is "non-A," or "A" is not "A." Father is made of non-father elements, including children. If there are no children, how can there be a father? Looking deeply into father, we see children; therefore, father is not father. The same is true with children, wife, husband, citizen, president, everyone, and everything.

In logic, the principle of identity is that "A" is "A" and "A" can never be "B." To free ourselves from our concepts, we have to transcend this principle. The first principle of the dialectics of prajñaparamita is that "A" is "non-A." Seeing that, we know that the well-being of "A" depends on the well-being of the "non-A" elements. The well-being of man depends on the well-being of non-man elements in nature. When you have a correct perception of man and know that man is made of non-man elements, it is safe to call man by his true names—trees, air, woman, fish, or man. The Buddha should be looked at in the same way. Buddha is made of non-Buddha elements. Enlightenment is made of non-enlightenment elements. Dharma is made of non-Dharma elements. Bodhisattvas are made of non-bodhisattva elements. These kinds of statements are in the *Prajñaparamita Diamond Sutra*, and they are the way to practice the second Door of Liberation, the door of signlessness.

If we learn the Three Doors of Liberation but don't practice them, they are of no use. To open the door of signlessness and enter the realm of suchness, reality, we have to practice mindfulness in our daily life. Looking deeply at everything, we see the nature of interbeing. We see that the president of our country is composed of non-president elements, including economics, politics, hatred, violence, love, and so on. Looking deeply into the person who is the president, we see the reality of our country and the world. Everything concerning our civilization can be found in him—our capacity to love, to hate, everything. One thing contains every other thing in it. We deserve our government and our president, because they reflect the reality of the country—the way we think and feel, and the way we live our daily lives. When we know that "A" is not "A," when we know that our president is not our president, that he is us, we will no longer reproach or blame him. Knowing that he is made only of non-president elements, we know where to apply our energies to improve our government and our president. We have to take care of the non-president and non-government elements within us and all around us. It is not a matter of debate. It is a matter of practice.

"In a place where there is something that can be distinguished by signs, in that place there is deception." Suddenly this sentence from the *Diamond Sutra* becomes clear. Until we look deeply into reality and discover its true nature of interbeing, we are fooled by signs or notions. When we see the signless nature of signs, we see the Buddha. After seeing the true nature of "A"—which is "non-A"—we touch the reality of "A." In Zen circles, it is said, "Before I began to practice, mountains were mountains and rivers were rivers. After I began to practice, mountains were no longer mountains and rivers were no longer rivers. Now, as I have practiced for some time, and mountains are again mountains and rivers are again rivers." This is not difficult to understand.

Notions, even notions of Buddha and Dharma, are dangerous. One Zen teacher was "allergic" to the word "Buddha," because he knew that many people misunderstood the Buddha. One day during a Dharma talk, he said, "I hate the word 'Buddha.' Every time I have to say it, I go to the river and rinse my mouth three times." Everyone in the assembly was silent, until one man stood up and said, "Teacher, I feel the same way. Every time I hear you say the word 'Buddha,' I have to go to the river and wash my ears three times." It means we have to transcend words, concepts, and notions, and enter the door of signlessness. "Kill the Buddha," is a drastic way of saying that we have to kill the concept of the Buddha to give the true Buddha a chance.

These teachings of the *Diamond Sutra* are closely related to those of the *Sutra on Knowing the Better Way to Catch a Snake*. We have to be careful not to get stuck, even to the teaching of the Buddha. "That is why we should not get caught up in dharmas or in the idea that this is not the Dharma," according to the *Diamond Sutra*. If you think the notion of dharma is dangerous, you may like the notion of non-dharma. But the notion of non-dharma is even more dangerous. This is what the Buddha means when he says, "Bhikkhus, all the teachings I give you are a raft. All teachings must be abandoned, not to mention non-teachings." You have to kill not only the teachings, but also the non-teachings, in order to have the true teaching. Even the Dharma has to be released, not to mention the non-Dharma.

The best way to practice is according to the spirit of non-practice, not clinging to forms. Suppose you practice sitting meditation very well. People look at you and see that you are a diligent practitioner. You sit perfectly, and you begin to feel a little proud. While others sleep late and do not come to the meditation hall on time, you are there sitting beautifully. With that kind of feeling in you, the happiness that results from your practice will be limited. But if you realize that you are practicing for everyone, even if the whole community is sleeping and you are the only one sitting, your sitting will benefit everyone and your happiness will be boundless. We should practice meditation this way—without form, in the spirit of non-practice.

The Buddha taught six *paramitas*, or perfections. The first is the practice of generosity, *dana. Danaparamita* should always be practiced without form. "If a bodhisattva practices generosity without relying on signs, the happiness that results cannot be conceived of or measured." When you volunteer to clean the kitchen or scrub the pots, if you practice as a bodhisattva, you will have great joy and happiness while doing so. But if you have the feeling, "I am doing a lot, and others are not contributing their fair share," you will suffer, because your practice is based on form and the discrimination between self and non-self.

When you are hammering a nail into a piece of wood, if you accidentally strike your finger, your right hand will put down the hammer and take care of your left hand. There is no discrimination: "I am the right hand giving you, the left hand, a helping hand." Helping the left hand is helping the right hand. That is practice without relying on form, and the happiness that results is boundless. It is the way a bodhisattva practices generosity and service. If we do the dishes with anger and discrimination, our happiness will be less than a teaspoonful.

The second paramita a bodhisattva practices is precepts, *silaparamita*. We should practice the precepts in this spirit also, without relying on form. We should not say, "I am practicing the precepts, not you. I work very hard to practice the precepts." There are those who eat a vegetarian diet without relying on form. They do not even have the idea that they are vegetarian and others are not. They only know that it is natural and enjoyable to be vegetarian. Precepts become protection and are no longer seen as a limitation of freedom.

This is true for the practice of the other paramitas—patience (*ksantiparamita*), energy (*viryaparamita*), and meditation (*dhyanaparamita*). The bodhisattva practices without relying on form. That is why his or her practice is a practice of non-practice. You practice and yet you do not look as though you are practicing. It is the deepest form of practice.

The sixth paramita is the practice of understanding, *prajñaparamita*. It is the basic paramita, sometimes described as the container carrying all the other paramitas. You need a good container to carry water, or the water will leak out. If you do not practice the perfection of understanding, you are like an unbaked earthen pot. The water will leak out and be lost. Prajñaparamita is also described as the mother of all buddhas and bodhisattvas. Those who practice looking deeply, vipasyana, are her children. These are important images from the *Prajñaparamita Sutras*.

The third Door of Liberation is wishlessness or aimlessness, *apranihita*. It means there is nothing to run after, nothing to attain or realize, nothing to be grasped. This is seen in many sutras, not only Mahayana ones, but in early sutras like the *Sutra on Knowing the Better Way to Catch a Snake*.

We all have the tendency to struggle in our bodies and our minds. We believe that happiness is possible only in the future. The realization that we have already arrived, that we don't have to travel any further, that we are already here, can give us peace and joy. The conditions for our happiness are already sufficient. We only need to allow ourselves to be in the present moment, and we will be able to touch them. What are we looking for to be happy? Everything is already here. We do not need to put an object in front of us to run after, believing that until we get it, we cannot be happy. That object is always in the future, and we can never catch up to it. We are already in the Pure Land, the Kingdom of God. We are already a Buddha. We only need to wake up and realize we are already here.

One of the basic teachings of the Buddha is that it is possible to live happily in the present moment. *Drishta dharma sukha vihari* is the expression in Sanskrit. The Dharma deals with the present moment. The Dharma is not a matter of time. If you practice the Dharma, if you live with and according to the Dharma, happiness and peace are with you right away. Healing takes place as soon as the Dharma is embraced.

In the teaching of Mahayana Buddhism, there are two dimensions of reality—the historical and the ultimate. In the historical dimension, it looks as though there is something to be realized. In the ultimate dimension, you are already what you want to become. We will understand more deeply the teaching of aimlessness when we come to the teaching of the *Lotus Sutra*.

PARALLAX PRESS
PO Box 7355
Berkeley CA 94707

Parallax Press publishes books and tapes on mindful awareness and social responsibility—"making peace right in the moment we are alive." It is our hope that doing so will help alleviate suffering and create a more peaceful world.

For our complete catalog of books and tapes, please send in this card.

Name _____

Address _____

City _____ State _____ Zip _____

Country _____

TWELVE

Sangha / Community

When I left the Temple of Complete Awakening in the highlands and returned to my community in Saigon, there were times I just called her name softly to relieve my loneliness. My Dharma brothers did not say anything. They were just there for me with their silent support.

If you have a supportive Sangha, it is easy to nourish your bodhichitta. If you do not have anyone who understands you, who encourages you in the practice of the living Dharma, your desire to practice may wither. Your Sangha—family, friends, and co-practitioners—is the soil, and you are the seed. No matter how vigorous the seed is, if the soil does not provide nourishment, your seed will die. A good Sangha is crucial for the practice. Please find a good Sangha or help create one.

Buddha, Dharma, and Sangha are three precious jewels in Buddhism, and the most important of these is Sangha. The Sangha contains the Buddha and the Dharma. A good teacher is important, but sisters and brothers in the practice are the main ingredient for success. You cannot achieve enlightenment by locking yourself in your room. Transformation is possible only when you are in touch. When you touch the ground, you can feel the stability of the earth and feel confident. When you observe the steadiness of the sunshine, the air, and the trees, you know that you can count on the sun to rise each day and the air and the trees to be there. When you build a house, you build it on solid ground. You need to choose friends in the practice who are stable, on whom you can rely.

Taking refuge in the Sangha means putting your trust in a community of solid members who practice mindfulness together. You do not have to practice intensively—just being in a Sangha where people are happy, living deeply the moments of their days, is enough. Each person's way of sitting, walking, eating, working, and smiling is a source of inspiration; and transformation takes place without effort. If someone who is troubled is placed in a good Sangha, just being there is enough to bring about a transformation. I hope communities of practice in the West will organize themselves as families. In Asian Sanghas, we address each other as Dharma brother, Dharma sister, Dharma aunt, or Dharma uncle, and we call our teacher Dharma father or Dharma mother. A practice community needs that kind of familial brotherhood to nourish our practice.

Two thousand, five hundred years ago, Shakyamuni Buddha proclaimed that the next Buddha will be named Maitreya, the "Buddha of Love." I think Maitreya Buddha may be a community and not just an individual. A good community is needed to help us resist the unwholesome ways of our time. Mindful living protects us and helps us go in the direction of peace. With the support of friends in the practice, peace has a chance.

Without a supportive Sangha, it would have been much more difficult for me to continue. She did not have a community like that, and it was difficult for her. The letters I sent to Hanoi were received, but the ones sent to Huê were not. I was not able to keep her apprised of the developments—that hundreds of young monks and nuns were being given new opportunities to practice and to help—and she began to feel isolated. During that time, my love for her was evolving. I began to see her everywhere. Every young monk and nun I encountered became a part of our love, and I felt that she, too, was a part of this transformation. I didn't realize how isolated she had become, not getting my letters.

Love has very much to do with bodhichitta. In my case, love had to do with the strong desire to become a monk, to practice for a whole generation and a whole society. In the beginning, there was attachment and inner conflict, but the conflict began to transform within twenty-four hours. On our second day together, already we talked only about continuing our practice as a monk and as a nun. Bodhichitta was our support and protection. Even the desire to knock on her door and ask her to come down to the sitting room to talk was overcome. We did not have to make any effort to practice the precepts. We just practiced them. Thanks to our bodhichitta, we followed the precepts quite naturally. It was bodhichitta that protected us.

When you are animated by bodhichitta, the strong desire to devote yourself to the practice of the Dharma for the well-being of many beings, that is all you need. Bodhichitta is a source of power within you. The best thing you can do for others is to help them touch the bodhichitta in themselves. The seed of bodhichitta is there; it is a matter of watering that seed and bringing it to life. One of the most important ways to nourish and protect bodhichitta is to find a good Sangha. If you have a Sangha that is joyful, animated by the desire to practice and help, you will mature as a bodhisattva. I always tell the monks, nuns, and lay practitioners at Plum Village that if they want to succeed in the practice, they have to find ways to live in harmony with one another, even with those who are difficult. If they cannot succeed in the Sangha, how can they succeed outside of it? Becoming a monk or a nun is not just between student and teacher. It involves everyone. Getting a "yes" from everyone in the Sangha is a true Dharma Seal.

In 1976, the communist government of Vietnam wanted to set up a government-supported Buddhist organization to replace the Unified Buddhist Church, and they spread a rumor that I had died of a heart attack in Paris. The young monks and nuns in Vietnam had strong faith in me. They knew I was doing my best to help and protect them. In Paris, through our office at the Peace Delegation of the Unified Buddhist Church, we stayed in touch with Amnesty International and other humanitarian organizations, and every time there were human rights violations by the government, such as the arrests of monks or nuns, we informed the press and others so they would intervene. That is one of the reasons the government decided to close down the Unified Buddhist Church and set up their own Buddhist organization. They had already arrested Thich Quang Do and Thich Huyen Quang, the leaders of the Unified Buddhist Church (who are still in prison, in 1995), and they wanted to confuse people and undermine the support that the people felt from us in Paris. When the rumor that I had died of a heart attack reached the nuns of Tu Nghiem Pagoda in Saigon, one young nun fainted.

Why do you faint, Sister? Many people have been killed while they were struggling for peace and social justice, but no one can destroy them. What exists cannot cease to exist, and what does not exist cannot come into being. Jesus, Gandhi, and Martin Luther King are still here, in us, in every cell of our bodies. If you hear the news again of my death, please smile. Your smile will prove your great understanding and your courage. There is no need to mourn, not only because the news is untrue, but because all of the young monks and nuns, animated by bodhichitta, can continue the practice without me.

Where is the self? Where is the non-self? Who is your first love? Who is the last? What is the difference between our first love and our last love? How can anything die? What is the connection between that nun at the Tu Nghiem Pagoda and my beloved, who was still in the nunnery in Huê? "Wherever there is form, there is deception." If you want to touch my love, please touch yourself.

Whether water is overflowing or evaporating depends on the season. Whether it is round or square depends on the container. Flowing in spring, solid in winter, its immensity cannot be measured, its source cannot be found. In an emerald creek, water hides a dragon king. In a cold pond, it contains the bright full moon. On the bodhisattva's willow branch, it sprays the nectar of compassion. One drop of water is enough to purify and transform the world in ten directions. Can you grasp water through form? Can you trace it to its source? Do you know where it will end? It is the same with your first love. Your first love has no beginning and will have no end. It is still alive, in the stream of your being. Don't believe it was only in the past. Look deeply into the nature of your first love, and you will see the Buddha.

When I found out that she was suffering, I invited her to join us, but she never got those letters either. Feeling abandoned, she lost energy, and eventually she left the order. Love is an accident, but we do not have to avoid or condemn love. The accident may cause us some suffering, but if we are strongly motivated by bodhichitta, the intention to bring happiness to many people, we have a Dharma protector and we will survive. With a good Sangha, you are better protected. When the arrow strikes, if you are surrounded by a supportive Sangha, you can continue your practice, and your love will be transformed. Without a good Sangha, you are vulnerable. Please do your best to set up a Sangha. A Sangha is a raft that can help you survive in turbulent moments. "I take refuge in the Sangha" is a strong pledge. With a good Sangha, you touch the Buddha, you touch the Dharma, and you touch yourself very deeply. It is thanks to the Sangha that I survived many difficult moments and have been able to be a resource for many people, including her.

THIRTEEN

The Avatamsaka Realm

The *Avatamsaka Sutra* is one of the most beautiful Buddhist scriptures. Avatamsaka means "flower ornament, garland, or wreath," or "decorating the Buddha with flowers." Isn't the Buddha beautiful enough? Why do we have to decorate him with flowers? The Buddha in this sutra is not just a person. He is more than a person.

The historical Buddha, Shakyamuni, was born 2,600 years ago in Kapilavastu, got married, had a child, left his family to practice, got enlightened, became a well-known teacher, helped many people, and died in Kushinagara at the age of eighty. One day, a disciple of his named Aniruddha was walking along the streets of Shravasti, when he was stopped by a group of monks from another sect. The monks asked him, "Will the Buddha exist after his death or cease to exist after his death?" During the lifetime of the Buddha, many people made efforts like that to try to understand the real Buddha. Aniruddha told them he did not know. Then, when he returned to the Jeta Grove and reported to the Buddha what had happened, the Buddha told him, "It is difficult to grasp the Buddha. When you see the Buddha in form, feelings, and perceptions, can you identify the Buddha through these things?" Aniruddha replied, "No, Lord." Then the Buddha asked, "Can you find the Buddha apart from form, perceptions, mental formations?" "No, Lord," he responded. The Buddha said, "I am in front of you and yet you cannot grasp me. How do you expect to get hold of me after I pass away?" The Buddha called himself *Tathagata*, "coming from suchness (reality as it is)," "going to suchness," or "one who comes from nowhere and goes nowhere," because suchness cannot be confined to coming or going.

When the monk Vakkali was dying in the home of a potter, the Buddha went to see him. When he arrived, Vakkali did his best to sit up, but the Buddha said, "No, Vakkali, please stay where you are." Then the Buddha asked him how he felt, how intense was his pain, and Vakkali said, "I have a lot of pain, Lord." The Buddha asked whether there was anything he regretted, and Vakkali said, "Lord, I only regret that I cannot come to see you more." The Buddha said, "Vakkali, if you practice my teaching, you are with me all the time. This body is not me." There are many stories like this in the scriptures. The Buddha is more than form. He is the living teaching. When you practice the way of the Buddha, you are transformed, and you are with the Buddha all the time.

Before passing away, the Buddha told his monks, "My friends, this is only my physical body. My Dharma body will be with you for as long as you continue to practice. Take refuge in the Dharma. Take refuge in the island of self. The Buddha is there." His statement was very clear.

If you touch the living Dharma body (*Dharmakaya*), you will not complain that you were born more than two thousand five hundred years after the Buddha and have no chance to see him or study with him. The Dharmakaya of the Buddha is always present, always alive. Wherever there is compassion and understanding, the Buddha is there, and we can see and touch him. Buddha as the living Dharma is sometimes called *Vairochana*. He is made of light, flowers, joy, and peace, and we can walk with him, sit with him, and take his hand. As we enter the realm of Avatamsaka, it is Vairochana Buddha we encounter.

In the Avatamsaka realm there is a lot of light. The Buddha and the bodhisattvas are all made of light. Let yourself be touched by the light, which is the enlightenment of the Buddha. Beams of light shining in every direction are pouring out from the pores of every enlightened being there. In the Avatamsaka realm, you become light, and you begin to emit light also. Allow yourself to be transformed by the light. Mindfulness is light. When you practice walking meditation alone, enjoying each step deeply, you emit the light of mindfulness, joy, and peace. Every time I see you walking like that, I am struck by one of the beams of light you are emitting, and suddenly I come back to the present moment. Then I, too, begin to walk slowly and deeply, enjoying each step. In the same way, you can allow yourself to be touched by the beams of light that are everywhere in the Avatamsaka realm. When you do, you will become a bodhisattva emanating light also. Let us enter the Avatamsaka realm together and enjoy it. Later, we can open the door for others to come, too.

Entering the Avatamsaka realm, we encounter a lot of space. The Avatamsaka realm is immense, without boundaries. There is enough space—inside and outside—for everyone, as the merit accumulated by the practice is enormous. Beings in the Avatamsaka realm never run out of space or time. That is why they have so much freedom. The Buddhas and bodhisattvas there welcome us and offer us infinite space. We feel very free and very much at ease in the Avatamsaka realm.

The third thing we see are flowers. Flowers are everywhere. Looking up, down, ahead, behind, to the left, and to the right, we see flowers. In fact, the eyes we see with become flowers, the ears we hear with are flowers, the lips we speak with become flowers, and the hands we receive tea with become flowers in the Avatamsaka realm. There are enormous lotus flowers—big enough for three or four people to sit on! Each of these lotus flowers has more than one thousand petals, and when we look deeply at one petal, we see that it, in itself, is another lotus flower with one thousand petals. And each of those petals is also a lotus of one thousand petals, and those lotuses are not smaller than the first lotus flower. It continues on like that forever. This may sound strange, but it is exactly what happens in the Avatamsaka realm. Here, we cannot say that one thing is bigger or smaller than another. The ideas of bigger and smaller are just not present, nor are the ideas of one and many. When we look into the second lotus and see one thousand petals, each of which is also a full lotus of one thousand petals, we see the many in the one and the one in the many, the miracle of interbeing.

What else do we see? We see vast oceans. The merit we acquire, the joy we savor, and the peace we experience are so vast that there is no other way to describe them. The word "ocean" is used many times in the Avatamsaka realm —ocean of merit, ocean of happiness, ocean of insight, ocean of vows. We vow to bring happiness to many people, and our vows are so huge that only an ocean can contain them. We experience peace and joy so large and intense that they can only be described in terms of oceans.

The Avatamsaka realm is also filled with precious gems —jewels of insight, understanding, and happiness. Everything we touch becomes a jewel for our enjoyment. We do not have to possess them, because every jewel is available for our delight. Everyone and everything here is a jewel. Every minute is a precious jewel, and in every jewel is a multitude of other jewels. We do not have to accumulate them. One jewel is enough, because in that world, each one contains all. The image of Indra's jeweled net is used in the *Avatamsaka Sutra* to illustrate the infinite variety of interactions and intersections of all things. The net is woven of an infinite variety of brilliant gems, each with countless facets. Each gem reflects in itself every other gem in the net, and its image is reflected in each other gem. In this vision, each gem contains all other gems. We do not need to be greedy here. One small jewel can satisfy us completely.

There are many beautiful clouds of different colors in the Avatamsaka world. In Buddhist sutras, clouds represent rain, and rain represents happiness. Without rain, nothing can grow. That is why we speak of Dharma rain, the rain of the colorful Dharma. Colorful rain and colorful clouds protect us and bring us a lot of joy and happiness. One of the ten stages a bodhisattva goes through is the "Dharma cloud stage," in which the bodhisattva makes many people happy with his or her Dharma rain.

In the Avatamsaka realm, we also find beautiful lion seats. Imagine beautiful, comfortable seats, fit for a lion, a great being that walks slowly with majesty, strength, and confidence. When we enter the Avatamsaka realm and see a bodhisattva walking like that, we feel inspired. Whenever we want to sit down, we find a lion seat beautifully crafted for us. We only have to sit there. There is nothing else to do. Our joy, peace, and happiness in the Avatamsaka realm are boundless.

There is also a beautiful parasol in the Avatamsaka realm that represents the warmth and enjoyment of the mindfulness we are dwelling in. When we are in mindfulness, at peace with ourselves, we dwell in warmth and enjoyment. Protected by mindfulness, we have deep insight and real peace. Entering the Avatamsaka realm, we encounter all these wonderful things.

When we arrive, we may wish to pay our respects to the Buddha. Let us enter chapter twenty of the *Avatamsaka Sutra* and look for the Buddha Shakyamuni. When we inquire about his whereabouts, someone tells us that he is in

Suyama Heaven in the palace, so we ask how to get there. But after we make just one or two steps in that direction, someone else points out to us that the Buddha is already here. We don't have to go to Suyama Heaven. And, indeed, we see Shakyamuni Buddha sitting under the bodhi tree right in front of us. We may have thought that Uruvela village was in India, on the planet Earth, but here in the Avatamsaka realm we also see the Buddha sitting under the bodhi tree with the children of Uruvela village.

Then someone from Suyama Heaven comes and tells us that the Buddha is in the Suyama Palace. This is confusing. How can a person be in two places at once? How can he be under the bodhi tree and in the Suyama Palace at the same time? But this is what happens in the Avatamsaka realm. Then another friend tells us that the Buddha is on Gridhrakuta, Vulture Peak, preaching the *Lotus Sutra* right now, not just 2,500 years ago. How can the Buddha be in three places at once? But soon we find that the Buddha is everywhere, at the same time! Things like that happen in the Avatamsaka realm. Because there is so much light, so much happiness, and so many jewels, it is possible for Shakyamuni to be everywhere at the same time.

In fact, not only Shakyamuni can perform that kind of miracle. Anyone in the Avatamsaka realm can do the same. We, too, can be everywhere at once. From any point in the cosmos, people can touch us wherever we are and wherever they are. We are not at all confined by time and space. We penetrate everywhere; we are everywhere. Whenever someone touches something with deep mindfulness, deep looking, he or she will touch us. It may sound strange, but in the Avatamsaka world, it is always that way.

Whenever I touch a flower, I touch the the sun and yet I do not get burned. When I touch the flower, I touch a cloud without flying to the sky. When I touch the flower, I touch my consciousness, your consciousness, and the great planet Earth at the same time. This is the Avatamsaka realm. The miracle is possible because of insight into the nature of interbeing. If you really touch one flower deeply, you touch the whole cosmos. The cosmos is neither one nor many. When you touch one, you touch many, and when you touch many, you touch one. Like Shakyamuni Buddha, you can be everywhere at the same time. Think of your child or your beloved touching you now. Look more deeply, and you will see yourself as multitudes, penetrating everywhere, interbeing with everyone and everything.

I have not been in Vietnam for more than twenty-five years, but several generations of young monks, nuns, and laypeople there have been touching me through my books and tapes, which are handwritten and circulated underground, and also through the practices of walking meditation and looking deeply. Through these things, I have been able to stay in touch with the people, the flowers, the trees, and the waters of Vietnam while touching the people, the flowers, the trees, and the waters of Europe and North America. In fact, just a clap of your hands is enough to touch myriad galaxies. The effect of one sound cannot be measured. Your every look, smile, and word reaches far-away universes and influences every living and non-living being in the cosmos. Everything is touching everything else. Everything is penetrating everything else. That is the world of Avatamsaka, and it is also our world. With deep looking and deep touching, we can transform this world into the world of Avatamsaka. The more we practice looking deeply, the more light is present, the more flowers there are, the more oceans, space, parasols, jewels, and clouds there are. It depends on us.

> When the Buddha emanates great light,
> the ten directions shine.
> Everyone in Heaven and Earth
> can see him freely, without obstruction.

When you emit light, you help people see, because your light wakes them up. The Buddha emanates great light, illuminating the ten directions. Everyone sees the Buddha freely, without obstruction.

> The Buddha is sitting in the Suyama Palace
> and yet he pervades all worlds in the cosmos.
> This is an extraordinary event,
> a cause of wonder to the whole world.

How can the Buddha sitting in the Suyama Palace be present everywhere in the cosmos? It is a miracle. But not only the Buddha can perform that miracle. All of us can also. We sit here, but our being, our presence pervades the whole cosmos. People with some insight and mindfulness can touch us wherever they find themselves. Just touch and you see. You feel what you want to touch, right there from where you are. Listen and recognize it within you. You do not have to read any text.

> All things have no provenance
> and no one can create them.
> There is nowhere whence they are born.
> They cannot be discriminated.

All things have no provenance. They have not come from anywhere, because they are free from the ideas of being and non-being. They do not have to be born. They cannot be grasped by our notions, or discriminated by our mental categories. They have come from nowhere; they will go nowhere. There is no author or creator. That is the true nature of reality. We can only touch and experience things when we are free from the concepts of birth and death, creator and created. All things have no provenance, therefore they have no birth. Because they have no birth, extinction cannot be found either. That is the way things are in the realm of Avatamsaka.

> All things are birthless and have no
> extinction either.
> Those who understand in this way
> will see and touch the Buddha.

If you penetrate the reality of no-birth and no-death, of the Dharma, of things, of reality, it is not difficult for you to touch the Buddha.

These verses are from chapter twenty. There are many equally beautiful verses to enjoy in the *Avatamsaka Sutra*, but since we know that touching one thing deeply, we touch the whole cosmos, we do not have to quote them all.

When we walk in the Avatamsaka realm, breathing in the Buddha, breathing out the Buddha, walking on the Buddha, and sitting on the Buddha, we are aware that the Buddha here is Vairochana, the living Dharma, reality as it is, suchness, and we are one with him. The Avatamsaka realm is so pleasant, and it is within our reach. It is a place we can step into the moment we want to, a world of light, oceans, Dharma clouds, jewels, lion seats, and flowers. It is available to us here and now. We need not waste a single moment of our life. We only have to step into the Avatamsaka realm to enjoy life thoroughly.

The Avatamsaka land is a product of our mind. Whether we live in the *saha* world filled with suffering, discrimination, and war, or whether we live in the Avatamsaka world filled with flowers, birds, love, peace, and understanding is up to us. The cosmos is a mental construction. Everything comes from our mind. If our mind is filled with afflictions and delusions, we live in a world of afflictions and delusions. If our mind is pure and filled with mindfulness, compassion, and love, we live in the Avatamsaka world.

In the *Avatamsaka Sutra*, the cosmos is described as a lotus flower with many petals, each of which is also a full lotus, the petals of which are also a full lotus, and so on. Whenever we see one thing in the Avatamsaka realm, we always find everything in the cosmos in it. The notions small and large do not exist here. When we stand facing the ocean, we may feel small and insignificant compared with the ocean. When we contemplate a sky filled with stars, we may have the impression we are nothing at all. But the thought that the cosmos is big and we are small is just an idea. It belongs to our mind and not to reality. When we look deeply at a flower, we can see the whole cosmos contained in it. One petal is the whole of the flower and the whole of the universe. In one speck of dust are many Buddha lands. When we practice that kind of meditation, our ideas about small, large, one and many will vanish.

The image of a flower representing the cosmos can teach us a lot. In the *Diamond Sutra*, we removed the distinction between self and non-self, person and non-person, living being and non-living being, and life span and non-life span. Now in the *Avatamsaka* realm, we discover that the so-called animate things are no different from inanimate things, that living things are made of non-living elements. Scientists are beginning to understand that what we thought to be inanimate actually contains life. We cannot draw a line between living things and non-living things. When we look at the Earth in that way, we see the whole planet as a living organism, and we can no longer distinguish between man and non-man, animals and vegetables, vegetables and minerals. We simply see the Earth as the beautiful body of a living being, and we know that any harm done to one part of that organism can harm the whole organism. It is like a flower or a human being. Anything done to one cell will affect the whole being. If you know that the Earth is a living organism, you will know how to protect her, because to protect the Earth and the air around the Earth is to protect ourselves. Everything is linked to everything else. To save our planet is to save ourselves, our children, and grandchildren. This idea is deep within the teaching of the Buddha. Buddhist monks and nuns are prohibited from burning vegetation, cutting down trees, or even cutting grass without a good motive.

In their daily chanting, Buddhist novices recite, "I will practice for the enlightenment of both living and non-living beings." This is a teaching from the *Diamond Sutra*. We protect the Earth because we are motivated by compassion and respect for all things, animate and inanimate. Those who have a desire to protect the Earth should study the *Diamond* and *Avatamsaka Sutras*. Seeing the cosmos as a flower is a wonderful image. In each flower, there are many petals, and in each petal, you can see the whole flower. The one is in the many and the many are in the one.

As a sixteen-year-old novice, I memorized the last verses of "Eulogies in the Palace of Suyama Heaven," from the *Avatamsaka Sutra*:

If people want to know
all Buddhas of all times,
they should contemplate the nature of the
cosmos:
All is but mental construction.

It's like a painter
spreading various colors.
Delusion grasps different forms,
but the elements have no distinctions.

In the elements, there is no form,
and no form in the elements.
And yet apart from the elements,
no form can be found.

In the mind is no painting.
In painting there is no mind.
Yet not apart from mind
is any painting to be found.

It depends on the way we see. The mind invents countless forms and ideas, and our world is a product of that kind of grasping. The elements—water, fire, earth, and space—and the form in your mind seem to be two different things. But if you look deeply, you see there is no form in your mind unless the elements are there, and there are no elements unless the forms are there. Forms and elements inter-are. One cannot be without the other.

That mind never stops
manifesting all forms,
countless, inconceivably many,
unknown to one another.

Just as a painter
can't know his own mind,
yet paints due to the mind,
so is the nature of all things.

A master painter may not know his own mind, but he draws from his own mind. The nature of phenomena in the world is like that. The nature of things (dharmas) is that they are born from our own mind. The world as it presents itself to us is a mental construction.

Mind is like an artist,
able to paint the worlds:
The five skandhas are born from the same
kind of functioning of the mind.
There is nothing it doesn't make.

If people know the way the mind functions
to create all kinds of worlds,
they will be able to see the Buddha
and understand the true nature of a Buddha.

This is a suggestion for us to find the best way to touch the Buddha—not to look for a person, a non-person, a name, a characteristic, prestige, or a tradition, but to observe our own mind and see how it functions.

The mind creates everything—our fear, our sorrow, birth, death, winning and losing, hell, love, hatred, despair, and discrimination. If we practice, we will understand the way the mind constructs things, and we will touch the Buddha.

When I was a young monk, I learned these verses by heart and chanted them every evening. Even though I practiced by rote, it helped water the seed of understanding, and slowly I began to understand. If you want to touch the Buddhas in the ten directions, the Buddhas of the three times, you have to look into the nature of the cosmos and discover that everything is a mental construction. The first teaching of the *Avatamsaka* is that everything is mind. Mind here does not mean mind consciousness, the intellect. It means something deeper, something individual and collective. Don't worry if you do not understand. You don't have to understand anything. Just enjoy the words of this beautiful sutra. If they make you feel lighter, that is enough. It is not necessary to feel a heavy weight on your shoulders. Someday, with no effort at all, you will understand. You only have to allow yourself to be there, to touch deeply each thing you encounter, to walk mindfully, and to help others with the whole of your being. This is the practice of non-practice. Straining your intellect only creates more obstacles. Listen deeply without using your intellect, and you will find yourself in the Avatamsaka world, touching light, jewels, and lotuses. When you are there, you only have to touch and be touched, and one day you will penetrate the truth of inter-being, and it will penetrate you.

FOURTEEN

The Lotus Sutra

The *Saddharma Pundarika Lotus Sutra* is the king of all Mahayana sutras. It provides the ground for reconciliation among Buddhists. In every tradition, people get stuck in their ways. They attach to a form and get bitten by the snake of misunderstanding. Each time, an effort is needed to renew the tradition, correcting the errors and introducing practices that are closer to the true teaching. The first Mahayana sutras tried to do this. The ideas of impermanence, non-self, and nirvana were presented in new ways to help people get closer to the original teaching of the Buddha. But, because they had difficulties being heard by the established communities of practice, the authors of these sutras often used language that was too strong. They said, for example, that *shravakas*, practicing only to get out of this world of suffering, not for the good and welfare of the many, were not truly the children of the Buddha.

In the *Vimalakirti Sutra*, the attack on the shravakas was like cannon fire. Shariputra, the most intelligent disciple of the Buddha, the big brother of all bhikkhus, was ridiculed, and, as a result, the whole congregation was humiliated. The point was to attack the tradition that considered

Buddhism as a way for only monks and nuns, for those who renounce the world. When the *Vimalakirti Sutra* appeared, Mahayana Buddhism was only a school of thought, not an established community. Their attitude was combative in order to make themselves heard. It was not until the second century that the *Lotus Sutra* provided Mahayanists with a ground to establish a real practice community.

In the *Lotus Sutra*, Shariputra returns to the forefront as Buddha's most beloved disciple. Shariputra sits next to the Buddha and receives his full attention. The Buddha tells him that he has not offered the *Lotus Sutra* before because the time was not ripe. Now, as the disciples have practiced and matured, they are ready to receive the deepest teaching.

The two main teachings of the *Lotus Sutra* are: (1) everyone has the capacity to become a fully enlightened Buddha, and (2) the Buddha is present everywhere, all the time. Before this, practitioners thought they could become an *arhat* and attain nirvana, extinguishing the fires of lust and afflictions, but they never imagined they could become a Buddha. They thought that to become an arhat was enough, because they only wanted to end their own suffering. The first aim of the *Lotus Sutra* was to abolish that attitude and to teach that everyone has the capacity to become a fully enlightened Buddha.

The second main teaching of the *Lotus Sutra* is that the life of the Buddha is not limited to eighty years or to India. You cannot say that the Buddha has been born or that he has died. He is here, forever. In the *Avatamsaka Sutra*, we have seen that the Buddha is not only Shakyamuni, but also Vairochana. Shakyamuni is one of the ways. Vairochana is the way.

In Buddhism, we sometimes speak of three vehicles (*triyana*)—the way of the shravakas (disciples), the way of the *pratyekabuddhas* (self-enlightened ones), and the way of the bodhisattvas. The aim of the *shravakayana* is to liberate oneself from the world of suffering and attain extinction of suffering. *Pratyekabuddhayana* is the vehicle of those who practice and get enlightened by penetrating the nature of interbeing. In the *bodhisattvayana*, you help everyone become enlightened. Before the *Lotus Sutra*, there were sharp distinctions among the three vehicles, and each vehicle would criticize the others as being too narrow, but in the *Lotus Sutra*, we learn that the three vehicles are one: "The Buddha, using skillful means, says that this is one way, this is another, and this is a third way for people to choose from, but, in fact, there is only one way (*ekayana*)." The term "ekayana," one vehicle, already appeared in the *Satipatthana Sutta* (Four Establishments of Mindfulness), and it is one of the key words in the *Lotus Sutra*. The *Lotus Sutra* says that no matter what tradition you belong to, you are a disciple of the Buddha. This is wonderful news! Today people in the West practice Theravada, Zen, Pure Land, Vajrayana, and many other Buddhist traditions, and we know that they are all practicing the true way of the Buddha. Thanks to the *Lotus Sutra*, peace and reconciliation among practitioners has become possible.

The *Lotus Sutra* has twenty-eight chapters. Please study the second chapter, "Skillful Means," carefully. There you will find the teaching that in all Buddha fields in the ten directions, all three vehicles—shravaka, pratyekabuddha, and bodhisattva—are, in fact, one, ekayana. The Buddha only presented them as three vehicles to help beings in certain stages of their practice. Ultimately, if an arhat is not animated by bodhichitta, he or she is not a true student of the Buddha, and not a real arhat.

In the third chapter, the Buddha predicts that Shariputra will become a fully enlightened Buddha, and everyone becomes so excited, they throw their *sanghati* robes into the air. Never before had the Buddha's disciples realized that they, too, could become fully enlightened Buddhas. After Shariputra is predicted to become a fully enlightened Buddha, he feels very self-confident, and then other disciples are also predicted by the Buddha to become fully enlightened Buddhas. The first teaching of the *Lotus Sutra* is that everyone can become a fully enlightened Buddha.

In the eleventh chapter, we find the second teaching— that the Buddha cannot be found in time and space, nor limited to time and space. In the first ten chapters, we have time and space. We see people who are not Buddhas practicing to become Buddhas. We are in the "historical dimension" of reality. From the eleventh chapter on, we enter the "ultimate dimension." In the historical dimension, you are born, you practice, you become enlightened, and you pass into mahaparinirvana. In the ultimate dimension, you are always in nirvana. You are already a Buddha.

There is nothing to be done. The *Lotus Sutra* has a wonderful way of showing us this truth.

The Buddha and all the disciples are sitting on Gridhrakuta, Vulture Peak, and the Buddha is preaching the *Lotus Sutra*. Suddenly they hear, "Wonderful! Wonderful! Shakyamuni Buddha is teaching the *Lotus Sutra*." Looking up, the entire assembly of monks, nuns, and bodhisattvas sees a beautiful stupa, a tower suspended in midair. The Buddha tells them, "Prabhutaratna, 'Abundant Treasures,' Buddha is here, witnessing our Dharma talk." In the *Lotus Sutra*, whenever people are touching the earth sitting on Gridhrakuta Mountain, they are in the historical dimension. When their attention is directed into space, they are searching for the ultimate dimension. But when they look up to see Prabhutaratna Buddha, they cannot see him. They are trying to see the ultimate through the eyes of history, through their views and notions. They are looking at the Buddha as a form. They see him in terms of time and space, and they don't touch his true nature as a Buddha. They cannot grasp, or they grasp too much, and that is why they cannot see the Buddha.

Shakyamuni Buddha explains that Prabhutaratna is a Buddha who realized full enlightenment a very long time ago and made a vow to come and utter, "Wonderful! Wonderful!" every time a Buddha appears in the world and teaches the *Lotus Sutra*. How can they see that Buddha? They can see the historical Buddha, but how can they see the ultimate Buddha, the Buddha unbound by time or space? Aware of the deep desire of the community, with endless compassion, Shakyamuni Buddha tries to help.

In former times, Prabhutaratna Buddha made a vow, "If any Buddha would like to open my stupa and see me, he or she will have to call back all his or her manifested bodies from the ten directions." Shakyamuni says, "I will try my best to do that," and he emits a powerful light from his forehead in all the ten directions. In an instant, the whole assembly is able to see countless Buddha lands all around, and in each Buddha land is a Shakyamuni Buddha teaching the *Lotus Sutra* to a large assembly. At that moment, the students of the Buddha realize that Shakyamuni Buddha is more than just one Buddha teaching on Earth, and more than just one person. They drop the notion that the Buddha is our Buddha, on our planet, our teacher, a human being with an eighty-year life span. Then the Buddha, sitting on Vulture Peak, smiles and calls all his manifested bodies back to the Earth, and within seconds countless Shakyamuni Buddhas are sitting together on Vulture Peak. The basic condition for opening the stupa of Prabhutaratna Buddha has been met. The Buddha goes to such lengths to help his disciples get rid of their notions and viewpoints.

Shakyamuni Buddha is then able to open the door of the stupa, but only a small number of those assembled are able to see into it and touch with their eyes Prabhutaratna Buddha as a reality. Most of the assembly is sitting at the foot of the mountain, and they cannot see anything. They are not at the same level. They are not yet free enough to touch the ultimate dimension. The bodhisattvas are capable of looking into the stupa and seeing the living

Prabhutaratna Buddha, but the shravakas down below cannot. The Buddha Shakyamuni, understanding their wish, uses his great power to lift them into the air so they are on the same level as the bodhisattvas and Buddhas, and all of them are able to look into the stupa and see Prabhutaratna Buddha. It means that with the support and help of the Buddha, we can rise above the ground we are sitting on—the ground of notions and concepts—and touch the ultimate dimension.

Each of us is in both the historical dimension and the ultimate dimension. But we have not yet learned to touch the ultimate dimension. We dwell only in the historical dimension. We need to practice in order to lift ourselves up, to abandon our attachment to the historical dimension, and to see into the true nature of no-birth, no-death, no up, no down, no one, and no many. From the standpoint of the historical dimension, Prabhutaratna Buddha is already in nirvana, so how can he be sitting there speaking? But in the ultimate dimension he is always there, saying, "Wonderful! Wonderful!" When everyone is lifted to the same level, they can all see Prabhutaratna Buddha in person, very alive and very beautiful, the Buddha who is not conditioned by time or space, the Buddha who is always there.

Next, Prabhutaratna Buddha, the Buddha of the ultimate dimension, makes room on his lion seat and invites Shakyamuni Buddha, the Buddha of the historical dimension, to come and sit next to him. Everyone sees that the two Buddhas, Shakyamuni and Prabhutaratna, are sitting on the same lion seat. The ultimate dimension and the historical dimension are not two, but one. It is Shakyamuni, the historical Buddha, who helps us touch the Buddha of the ultimate dimension. We cannot say that the Buddha has a beginning or an end. He has been a Buddha for a long time and will be a Buddha for a long time. This is the second main teaching of the *Lotus Sutra*.

Sitting on Vulture Peak, we are still in the historical dimension. Suddenly we hear, "Wonderful! Wonderful!" and the ultimate is touching us. We look up and see the stupa of the immortal Buddha, Prabhutaratna, and we lift our eyes to see him. This is our first glimpse of the ultimate. We very much want to open the door of the stupa and see the Buddha of the ultimate directly, but there is a long way to go and we need the help of our teacher. The door is closed, preventing us from seeing the ultimate reality. What is the door? It is our ignorance, notions, discriminations, and views. The door of the stupa is in every one of us. Our teacher, Buddha Shakyamuni, tries to help us, saying, "To open this door, I need to call back all my transformed bodies who are everywhere in the cosmos. When they are back here on Vulture Peak, I will be able to open the door of the stupa." So he emits light in the ten directions, and we see many Buddha lands, and Shakyamuni Buddha is teaching in each of them. Now we can drop our view of Shakyamuni as one person. All these Buddhas are Shakyamuni, and all of them are on lotus seats preaching the *Saddharma Pundarika Sutra*.

The door is now opened, but conditions are still not ripe for us to see Prabhutaratna Buddha. Buddhas and bodhisattvas can see him through that door, but we cannot because we are sitting in another land. The Buddha knows our wish, and with his mind, he lifts us slowly into the air. It means we have to transcend the historical dimension to be equal with the Buddhas and bodhisattvas, who are in endless space, the ultimate dimension. Then we can look into the stupa and see Prabhutaratna Buddha.

If we still have the idea that Prabhutaratna Buddha and Shakyamuni Buddha belong to different worlds, that the Buddha of the ultimate dimension and the Buddha of the historical dimension are two, not one, that view is overcome when, suddenly, we see Prabhutaratna Buddha make room on his lion seat for Shakyamuni to sit near to him. What else can the Buddha do to help us see?

The *Lotus* and *Avatamsaka Sutras* are two of the finest books of poetry ever written. As far as the poetic imagination is concerned, no one has surpassed the Indian mind. The Indians used their imaginations to express the deepest insight. Just the image of Prabhutaratna Buddha and his stupa already conveys a lot. At that time in India, plays like the *Mahabharata* were very much enjoyed, and they influenced the way of presenting the teaching. That is one reason the *Saddharma Pundarika*, *Vimalakirti*, and other sutras were presented like plays. Please allow yourself to touch the Buddha's teaching through this imagery, poetry, and dialogue.

In the fifteenth chapter of the *Lotus Sutra*, something wonderful happens. Bodhisattvas from many lands come and greet Shakyamuni Buddha, and tell him, "Master, we have come to help you with the teaching, because the need here is so great." The Buddha responds, "Thank you, but we already have enough bodhisattvas in this Buddha land. You may go back to your own lands and help there." The Buddha is expressing confidence in his earthly disciples, and that includes you. Then he emits more light, and the earth cracks, allowing countless bodhisattvas to emerge from the earth, all of them very beautiful in their appearance and their way of speaking and teaching. They approach the Buddha, bow deeply, and say, "Master, we are capable of taking care of this land. We do not need other bodhisattvas. They can teach in their own lands." The Buddha replies, "Yes, you are right. There are enough teachers already here to take care of this Earth." And then, thanking the bodhisattvas who have come from other worlds, he says, "You may go home. You are needed in your own countries."

It is very much like the situation today. Many bodhisattva teachers are springing up in the West. Whenever we have a Lamp Transmission Ceremony at Plum Village, authorizing someone to teach the Dharma, it is a joyful occasion, confirming that bodhisattva teachers are springing up in this very land. We have to support these bodhisattvas. Every time a bodhisattva emerges from the Earth, I am very happy, and all of us feel encouraged. At Plum Village, hundreds of thousands of daffodils appear on a hillside in the Upper Hamlet every March. The first time I saw so many thousands of beautiful golden daffodils spring up from the earth like that, I thought of this image from the *Lotus Sutra*, and we named that hillside "Treasure of the *Dharmakaya*."

Shariputra then asks the Buddha, "Lord, you were enlightened at the age of thirty-five and have taught for only forty-five years. How is it that you have so many brilliant students, bodhisattvas from all over the cosmos? It would be like a young man of twenty-five having seventy or eighty children." The Buddha said, "You do not understand, because you only see me in the historical dimension. When you see me in the ultimate dimension, you will understand how I have millions of disciples capable of taking care of this Earth and many other realms as well."

In chapter twenty-three of the *Lotus Sutra*, we enter a third dimension, that we can call the dimension of action. Buddhas and bodhisattvas come from the ultimate dimension to the historical dimension in order to act, to help, to do what needs to be done. The first bodhisattva we see in this dimension is called Medicine King. His practice is to inhabit whatever kind of body is needed to be of help. When the body of a politician, a policeman, a man, or a woman is needed, he inhabits that. Each of us has many kinds of bodies, and Medicine King Bodhisattva shows us how to use the one that is most needed in each situation to bring about healing. His is the way of devotion, trust, and love; he never abandons anyone or anything.

In chapter twenty-four, we encounter Wonderful Sound Bodhisattva, who practices the samadhi of using whatever language is appropriate to help living beings. When living beings speak in the language of signs, he speaks in the language of signs. When they speak in the language of psychology, he speaks in the language of psychology. When they speak the language of sex or drugs, he speaks in the language of sex and drugs in order to help. In his past lives, Wonderful Sound Bodhisattva used music to make offerings to Buddhas. He has come to our world from the ultimate dimension, speaking many languages and using music in order to establish real communication.

Then we encounter Avalokiteshvara Bodhisattva, a child of the Earth, representing the kind of action that our Earth needs most, the energy of love. When you love, you want to be fully present in order to offer your support. The Buddha says, "Anyone who hears the name of Avalokiteshvara will overcome all suffering." Avalokiteshvara teaches the art of deep listening. If you practice that art, you overcome a lot of pain and suffering. When you are in hell, consumed by anger and hatred, if you touch Avalokiteshvara in your heart, the fires will be turned into cool, refreshing water. When you are drowning in the ocean of suffering, facing countless storms and demons, if you evoke the name of Avalokiteshvara, your suffering will be transformed, you will be saved. When you are bound in chains, if you practice the mindfulness of Avalokiteshvara, you will be liberated. When you feel others trying to destroy you with poisons, if you touch the love in yourself, you will not be harmed. No matter where you are, you can touch Avalokiteshvara with his wonderful capacity of being there.

Avalokiteshvara has realized these five contemplations: (1) The contemplation of looking deeply, vipasyana; seeing the real; breaking through illusions, notions, and concepts; and getting to suchness, which is free of all ideas. (2) The contemplation of pure heart and mind. When notions and afflictions are dissolved, we enter pure, undeluded mind. (3) The contemplation on immense understanding, prajñaparamita, touching the nature of emptiness and interbeing. (4) The contemplation on compassion, *karuna*, looking into the suffering of people and finding ways to transform their pain. (5) The contemplation on love, *maitri*, looking into others, knowing what to do to bring them happiness, and offering that. Avalokiteshvara is always there. Whenever we need him, we can touch him by practicing looking deeply, pure heart and mind, immense understanding, compassion, and love.

We can enter the *Lotus Sutra* through three doors. The first is through the historical dimension, the dimension of forms, signs, and phenomena. The second is through the ultimate dimension, the dimension of substance, nature, and noumena. The third is through the dimension of action, where we try to serve, guided by so many exemplary bodhisattvas. If you have the opportunity to read, study, and practice this wonderful sutra, I know you will find it a pleasure.

FIFTEEN

A Walk in the Ultimate Dimension

In the *Diamond Sutra*, the Buddha says, "In a place where something can be distinguished by signs, in that place there is deception." Still, we stick to signs and lose the essence, which is interbeing, signlessness, and emptiness. Caught in signs, we forget that reality is neither self nor non-self, person nor non-person, living being nor non-living being, life span nor non-life span. Our practice is to look deeply and to live deeply, dwelling in the "diamond samadhi" (vajra-chedika prajñaparamita concentration). We stay concentrated not only while practicing sitting meditation, but also while walking, drinking tea, or holding our newborn baby. Looking deeply, we are not fooled by signs.

While telling the story of my first love, I have done my best to dwell in that kind of samadhi, to stay in touch with reality. I hope you have been practicing the same. The story took place forty-five years ago, but if you look through the eyes of the *Diamond Sutra*, we will know that because she is made of non-person elements, we can touch her here and now. When you touch a flower in diamond samadhi, you touch the sun and the whole cosmos! If you penetrate the interbeing nature of the flower, you touch everything. You do not have to ask, "What happened next?" because you see all of eternity right before your eyes. You touch one thing deeply, and everything is there. If you are in a Sangha practicing like this, living and touching deeply, the practice is very easy. Don't worry if you still do not understand. Just allow the Dharma rain to continue moistening the soil of your store consciousness. Although the Dharma is offered using concepts, it is possible to receive it without getting stuck in concepts.

When we look at the vast ocean, we see many waves. We may describe them as high or low, big or small, vigorous or less vigorous, but these terms cannot be applied to water. From the standpoint of the wave, there is birth and there is death, but these are just signs. The wave is, at the same time, water. If the wave only sees itself as a wave, it will be frightened to death. The wave must look deeply into herself in order to realize that she is, at the same time, water. If we take away the water, the wave cannot be; and if we remove the waves, there will be no water. Wave is water, and water is wave. They belong to different levels of being. We cannot compare the two. The words and concepts that are ascribed to the wave cannot be ascribed to water.

Reality cannot be described by words or notions. Nirvana is the extinction, first of all, of notions. In the Avatamsaka realm, we do not look for Shakyamuni Buddha as a form. We look for Vairochana Buddha, who is the substance of Shakyamuni and all other Buddhas of the past, present, and future, which is to say our own substance, because we are all Buddhas. In the Avatamsaka realm, space is also time. The past is looking at the future and smiling, the future is looking at the past and smiling, and both can be found and touched in the present.

When you step into the Avatamsaka realm, you are a Buddha. You don't have to say that you are a future Buddha, because past, present, and future are one. When you are capable of touching the water, it is wonderful, but it does not mean the wave has vanished. The wave is *always* the water. If you try to touch only the wave and not the water, you will suffer from fear of birth and death and many other afflictions. But if you look deeply into yourself and realize that you are the water, all fear and afflictions will vanish. Touching the water, you also touch the wave. When you enter the Avatamsaka realm and touch Vairochana, you also see Shakyamuni sitting under the bodhi tree. Vairochana and Shakyamuni Buddha are one, like water and wave.

Since the reality of Vairochana cannot be described in words or concepts, it can be dangerous to use words or concepts to talk about it. Nirvana is a safe way to describe Vairochana, because nirvana means the extinction of all ideas and concepts. In some traditions, the word "Father" is used, but we have to ask, Why father and not mother? Any term that evokes its opposite can be problematic. God the Mother is a good phrase to neutralize any ideas we may have about God the Father.

This poem to a dahlia was written by a young poet in Vietnam. His name is Quach Thoai:

Standing quietly by the fence,
you smile your wondrous smile.
Surprised, I remain speechless.
I hear you sing a song
that began I know not when.
I bow deeply.

A dahlia is an ordinary flower we can see every day, but if we are not attentive, we will miss it. That morning the poet was fully present, able to touch the flower. The flower's song has always been there. Suddenly, the poet was able to step into the realm of Vairochana, the Dharmakaya Buddha, and hear the song of the flower. Out of respect he bowed deeply. The dahlia is Vairochana Buddha, who is teaching all the time, with compassion. Because we get caught in forgetfulness, we are not able to hear the Buddha teaching, but it does not mean he is not there. In fact, everything—the grass, the flowers, the leaves, and the pebbles—is always expounding the *Saddharma Pundarika Lotus Sutra*.

There is a chapter in the *Avatamsaka Sutra* about the practice of Samantabhadra, the Bodhisattva of Universal Goodness. Samantabhadra Bodhisattva is sitting in front of Shakyamuni Buddha and he enters into a samadhi called "The Concentration of the Immanent Body," the Vairochana body of all Buddhas. In that samadhi, he touches the true body of all Buddhas and steps into the world of Avatamsaka. Although he is sitting in front of Shakyamuni

Buddha, countless Buddhas appear to him, and in front of each Buddha is another Samantabhadra Bodhisattva.

If you practice one hour of sitting or walking like that, entering into the realm of the Avatamsaka and looking at everything in that way to discover the Vairochana Immanent Body of All Buddhas, you touch countless Buddhas of the past, present, and future and hear Dharma talks given by each of them. When the young Vietnamese poet suddenly entered the Avatamsaka realm and met a Buddha called "dahlia," he listened to the Dharma talk given by the Buddha Dahlia, and moved, he bowed to the dahlia. The Buddha is always teaching. Times are teaching, lands are teaching, living beings are teaching. If you have an attentive ear, you can hear the authentic Dharma all the time.

The future is the past and the present is the future. The three times look to each other and awaken the world in infinite ways. There are no boundaries to the means of total knowledge. In the world of Avatamsaka, space is made of time and time is made of space. One particle of space contains the totality of space. One particle of space contains the totality of time. One particle of time contains the totality of time. One particle of time contains all space and all time. To begin this practice, look into the nature of impermanence. Then continue and look into the nature of non-self and interbeing. Just by doing that, everything will be revealed to you in its entirety, the one in the many and the many in the one.

In the Avatamsaka realm, we learn that everything is a construction of our mind. When we are caught by notions, when we have so much ignorance and affliction in ourselves, we cannot see the true nature of things, and we construct a world full of suffering. We build prisons, we build hell, we build racial discrimination. We pollute the environment because we lack the insight of interbeing. The world constructed by the deluded mind is a world full of hatred, suffering, and delusion.

If we practice looking deeply, vipasyana, we see into the true nature of interbeing, and our ignorance is transformed into insight. If after reading the *Avatamsaka Sutra*, you go out for walking meditation, the world will be a little brighter. There will be more light, more space, more flowers, and more oceans. There will be more birds singing and more time for you to enjoy them. That is also a production of mind. If we continue looking deeply together, we will be able to produce the Avatamsaka world right now. That is the best way to reduce suffering. To reduce suffering means to reduce the amount of ignorance, the basic affliction within us. Everything penetrates everything else. To harm one person is to harm ourselves and all people at the same time. To bring relief to one person, is to bring relief to everyone, including ourselves. This insight brings about the kinds of action that are truly helpful, the great actions performed by Samantabhadra Bodhisattva.

In the Avatamsaka realm, time is endless. Over here, we run out of time, but there, you never run out of time. And you have so much space. Space there is made of time, and time of space. Here, we have the notion of a life span. We

think that before we were born, we did not exist, and after we die, we will no longer be. With our notion of life
span, we don't have much time. But there, the notion of
life span has been removed, and there is only freedom.

Some people ask whether in the Avatamsaka world you
can find coffee or Coca-Cola. Yes, these things exist there,
but there are so many other, more enjoyable things that
people don't need Coca-Cola. People don't need drugs.
The sunshine, the clouds, the flowers, the gems are so enjoyable you don't have to look for means to forget. Here
you may want to take refuge in something to help you forget reality. When your spouse causes you a lot of suffering,
you take refuge in your studies or your work, perhaps your
social or environmental work. You drink alcohol because
you want to forget, to escape. You use drugs to flee from a
reality that is not pleasant. But in the Avatamsaka realm,
things are so pleasant you don't need these things. It's not
that they are forbidden. If you want to find them, you can
find them, but you don't need them. If we bring people
who are enemies into the Avatamsaka realm, they will be-
have like Buddhas. They will benefit from the light, the
space, and the time, and they won't do what they are doing here.

One autumn day, I was practicing walking meditation.
The leaves were falling just like rain. I stepped on one leaf,
and I stopped, picked it up, looked at it, and smiled, realizing that that leaf has always been there. Every autumn
the leaves fall, and every spring they remanifest themselves.
They stay throughout the summer, and then in autumn,

they fall to the ground again. They are playing hide-and-seek, pretending to die and to be reborn, but it is not true. When I looked deeply into the leaf, I saw that it was not just one leaf, just as the Buddha is not just one person. The Buddha is, at the same time, everywhere. We learned that in the *Avatamsaka* and *Lotus Sutras*. The leaf, too, was everywhere. I asked the leaf to call back all its manifestations. Because the leaf was free from notions of birth and death, it was able to do so.

Seven years after the death of my mother, I woke up suddenly one night, went outside, and saw the moon shining brightly. At two or three o'clock in the morning, the moon is always expressing something deep, calm, and tender, like the love of a mother for her child. I felt bathed in her love, and I realized that my mother is still alive and will always be alive. A few hours earlier, I had seen my mother very clearly in a dream. She was young and beautiful, talking to me, and I talked to her. Since that time, I know that my mother is always with me. She pretended to die, but it is not true. Our mothers and fathers continue in us. Our liberation is their liberation. Whatever we do for our transformation is also for their transformation, and for our children and their children.

When I picked the autumn leaf and looked at it, I could smile, because I saw the leaf calling back a multitude of her bodies in the ten directions, just as Shakyamuni Buddha did in the *Lotus Sutra*. Then I looked at myself, and saw myself as a leaf, calling back countless bodies of mine to be with me at that moment. We can do that by dissolving the idea that we are only here and now. We are simultaneously everywhere, in all times.

When you touch the soil here, you touch the soil there also. When you touch the present moment, you touch the past and the future. When you touch time, you touch space. When you touch space, you touch time. When you touch the lemon tree in early spring, you touch the lemons that will be there in three or four months. You can do that because the lemons are already there. You can touch the lemon tree in the historical dimension or the ultimate dimension; it is up to you. The practice of the *Lotus Sutra* is to touch yourself, the leaf, and the tree in the ultimate dimension.

When you touch the wave, you touch the water at the same time. That is our practice. If you are with a group of friends practicing mindfulness while sitting, walking, or drinking tea, you will be able to touch the ultimate dimension while living in the historical dimension. Your fear, anxiety, and anger will be transformed easily when you are not confined by the waves, when you are able to touch the water at the same time.

The world of peace and joy is at our fingertips. We only need to touch it. When I enter the Plum Village kitchen, I may ask a student, "What are you doing?" If she says, "Thây, I am cutting some carrots," I will feel a little disappointed. I want her to leave the historical dimension and touch the ultimate dimension. She only needs to look up and smile. Or if she was thinking of something else and was brought back to the present moment by my question, she might look up and say, "Thank you," or "I am breathing." Those are good answers. You do not have to die to enter the Kingdom of God. In fact, you have to be alive to do so. What makes you alive? Mindfulness. Everything around you and in you can be the door to enter the *Dharmadhatu*. When you practice walking meditation, ask a tree or a flower to tell you about the Avatamsaka realm. I am sure it will show you the way in.

In *The Stranger*, Albert Camus tells us about a man named Meursault, who is in prison. In his cell one day, Meursault was able to touch life, to touch the Avatamsaka realm. Lying flat on his back, he looked up, and, through a small window near the ceiling, he *saw* the blue sky for the first time in his life. How could a grown man see the blue sky for the first time? In fact, many people live like that, imprisoned in their anger, frustration, or belief that happiness and peace are only in the future. Meursault had three days to live before his execution. In that moment of mindfulness, the sky was really there and he was able to touch it. He saw that life had meaning, and he began living deeply the moments that were left for him. The last three days of his life became true life.

On the last day, a priest knocked at his cell door to extract a confession from him, but Meursault refused. Finally the priest left, frustrated. At that moment, Meursault described the priest as someone who lives like a dead person. *"Il vit comme un mort."* Meursault realized that it was the priest who needed to be saved, not him. If we look around, we see many people who are like dead persons, carrying their own dead bodies on their shoulders. We need to do whatever we can to help them. They need to be touched by something—the blue sky, the eyes of a child, an autumn leaf—so they can wake up.

When I was a little boy, I read a novel about a French hunter who got lost in an African jungle. He thought that he was going to die, because he could not find his way out. But he was adamant that he would not pray to God. So he did something that was half-praying and half-joking: *"Dieu, si tu existes, viens à mon secours!"* (God, if you exist, come and rescue me!) A few minutes later, an African showed himself and helped him out. Later he wrote, *"J'ai appelé Dieu, et il m'est arrivé un nègre."* (I called God, but a Negro came.) He did not know that the African *was* God. In the case of Meursault, God came to rescue him in the form of a piece of blue sky. We might be saved by a flower, a pebble, a bird, or a thunderclap. Anything can bring us a message from Heaven, from the Avatamsaka realm. Anything can wake us up to life right here and right now. We should not discriminate.

When I picked up the leaf, I saw that the leaf was pretending to be born in the springtime and pretending to die at the end of autumn. We too appear, manifest to help living beings including ourselves, and then disappear. We have within us a miraculous power, and if we live our daily lives in mindfulness, if we take steps mindfully, with love and care, we can produce the miracle and transform our world into a miraculous place to live. Taking steps slowly, in mindfulness, is an act of liberation. You walk and you free yourself of all worries, anxieties, projects, and attachments. One step like this has the power to liberate you from all afflictions. Just being there, you transform yourself, and your compassion will bear witness.

Look at the flowers, butterflies, trees, and children with the eyes of compassion. This is a deep practice, taught in the *Lotus Sutra*. The energy of compassion in you will transform life and make it more beautiful. Compassion is always born of understanding, and understanding is the result of looking deeply.

> Walking joyfully in the ultimate dimension,
> walk with your feet,
> not with your head.
> If you walk with your head, you'll get lost.

> Teaching Dharma in the ultimate dimension,
> falling leaves fill the sky.
> The path is covered with autumn moonlight.
> The Dharma is abundant in all directions.

> Discussing Dharma in the ultimate dimension,
> we look at each other and smile.
> You are me, don't you see?
> Speaking and listening are one.

Enjoying lunch in the historical dimension,
I feed all generations of ancestors
and all future generations.
Together, we will find our way.

Getting angry in the historical dimension,
we close our eyes and look deeply.
Where will we be in three hundred years?
We open our eyes and hug.

Resting in the ultimate dimension,
using snowy mountains as a pillow
and beautiful pink clouds as blankets.
Nothing is lacking.

Meditating in the ultimate dimension,
sharing Prabhutaratna's lion seat,
every moment is a realization
every fruit is ripe and delicious.

Notes

Most Mahayana Buddhist texts were originally recorded in Sanskrit, so technical Buddhist terms in this book are rendered in Sanskrit. When they are also given in another language such as Pali, Japanese, or Chinese, that is noted.

There are many important texts and translations in English on Buddhism in general and on Mahayana Buddhism in particular. Following are a few key references for the sutras cited in this book:

CHAPTER THREE — *The Advent of Mahayana Buddhism*
The *Ugradatta Sutra* can be found in *Taisho Revised Tripitaka*, number 322. It is sutra 19 in the *Maharatnakuta*, a sutra collection, a selection from which can be found in Garma C. C. Chang, editor, *A Treasury of Mahayana Sutras* (Pennsylvania State University Press, 1983).

The *Vimalakirti Nirdesha Sutra*, *Taisho Revised Tripitaka*, number 475, can be found in English in Robert Thurman, *The Holy Teaching of Vimalakirti* (Pennsylvania State University Press, 1976).

CHAPTER FIVE — *The Better Way to Catch a Snake*
The *Sutra on Knowing the Better Way to Catch a Snake* is available in both Pali and Chinese. In Pali, it is the *Alagaddupama Sutta* ("Snake Simile," *Majhima Nikaya*, number 22). In Chinese, it is the *Arittha Sutra* (*Madhyama Agama*, number 220, *Taisho Revised Tripitaka*, num-

ber 26). It has been translated into English, with commentary, by Thich Nhat Hanh in *Thundering Silence* (Parallax Press, Berkeley, 1993).

CHAPTER SEVEN — *The Diamond That Cuts through Illusion*

The *Diamond Sutra* can be found in *Taisho Revised Tripitaka* number 235. It has been translated into English, with commentary by Thich Nhat Hanh, in *The Diamond That Cuts through Illusion* (Parallax Press, Berkeley, 1992). For a discussion on emptiness, see Thich Nhat Hanh, *The Heart of Understanding* (Parallax Press, Berkeley, 1988).

CHAPTER NINE — *Three Dharma Seals*

The *Sutra on the Dharma Seal* can be found in *Taisho Revised Tripitaka*, number 104. It has been translated into English by Thich Nhat Hanh in the *Plum Village Chanting and Recitation Book* (Parallax Press, Berkeley, 1995).

The *Hundred Parables Sutra* can be found in the Koryo edition of the Buddhist canon, Kuan section. It has been translated into English by Kazuaki Tanahashi in *Garland of Fools* (unpublished manuscript).

CHAPTER THIRTEEN — *The Avatamsaka Realm*

The *Aniruddha Sutta* can be found in *Samyutta Nikaya* 22, 6. It has been translated from Pali into English by Thich Nhat Hanh in the *Plum Village Chanting and Recitation Book* (Parallax Press, Berkeley, 1995).

Some of the quotations from *The Avatamsaka Sutra* are directly from the Chinese and some are adapted from Thomas Cleary, *The Flower Ornament Scripture* (Shambhala Publications, Boston, 1993). See especially pages 442–445.

CHAPTER FOURTEEN — *The Lotus Sutra*

There are many translations of the *Lotus Sutra* into English. One is *The Lotus Sutra*, translated by Burton Watson (Columbia University Press, New York, 1993). Another is *Scripture of the Lotus Blossom of the Fine Dharma*, translated by Leon Hurvitz (Columbia University Press, New York, 1976).

Parallax Press publishes books and tapes on Buddhism and related subjects to make them accessible and alive for contemporary readers. It is our hope that doing so will help alleviate suffering and create a more peaceful world.

We carry all books and tapes of Thich Nhat Hanh. For a copy of our free catalog, please write:

Parallax Press
P.O. Box 7355
Berkeley, CA 94707